D1479173

CLUES

TO
AFRICA,
ISLAM, &
THE GOSPEL

This is by no means a definitive study of Islam in Africa. Yet despite its brevity, or perhaps because of it, Colin Bearup's little book deserves to be widely circulated and read by North American Christians and missionaries who on this continent imbibe a media-and-politics-driven view of Islam that is dread-driven, factually distorted, and deeply antithetical to the nonnegotiable mandate of our Lord to love neighbors and welcome strangers—including Muslims. Colin Bearup is to be congratulated for writing both knowledgeably and accessibly on this important subject.

JONATHAN BONK
director, *Dictionary of African Christian Biography*
mission research professor, Boston University

Readers will discover here a treasure trove of insights into how to relate well to and share the gospel with African Muslims. This is above all a practical manual for understanding how Islam affects the everyday life of its African followers and learning how to be a credible witness among them for Christ. Colin Bearup has written a must-read primer for every Christian worker serving God among African Muslims.

DR. RICHARD HIBBERT
director of the Centre for Cross-Cultural Mission, Sydney Missionary & Bible College
author of *Walking Together on the Jesus Road: Discipling in Intercultural* Contexts

This book is an essential read and study guide for any contemplating church-planting ministry in Africa, especially where there are Muslim communities. It is erudite, easy to grasp, challenging, and insightful, with short chapters based on acute observation and years of practical ministry in Africa and digs deep into the quirks of theology and culture we unwittingly carry with us into a Muslim African context. This is an essential eye-opener for any considering church-planting ministry in Africa.

PATRICK JOHNSTONE
WEC International
author emeritus, *Operation World*

I didn't expect to read anything more than a rehash of what has already been written in the last three decades by many focused on Muslims—the ultimate challenge to the Lordship of Christ Jesus. However, to my delight, I discovered that C. J. Bearup has some very significant insights that penetrate the "Gordian knot" regarding disciple-making among African Muslims that lasts. The best recommendation I can make is this: After over fifty years of focus on the Great Commission among Muslims, I would truly like to sit and learn from this man.

DR. GREG LIVINGSTONE
founder, Frontiers

CLUES

TO AFRICA, ISLAM, & THE GOSPEL

Insights for New Workers

Colin Bearup

WILLIAM CAREY PUBLISHING

Available at missionbooks.org

Clues to Africa, Islam, and the Gospel: Insights for New Workers

© 2020 by Colin Bearup

Scripture taken from the Holy Bible, NEW INTERNATIONAL VERSION®, NIV® Copyright © 1973, 1978, 1984, 2011 by Biblica, Inc.® Used by permission. All rights reserved worldwide.

Published by William Carey Publishing
10 W. Dry Creek Cir
Littleton, CO 80120 | www.missionbooks.org

William Carey Publishing is a ministry of Frontier Ventures
Pasadena, CA 91104 | www.frontierventures.org

Mike Riester, cover and interior design
Cover image from unsplash.com
Andrew Sloan, copyeditor

ISBNs: 978–1-64508–252–1 (paperback),
        978–1-64508–254–5 (mobi),
        978–1-64508–255–2 (epub)

Printed Worldwide

24 23 22 21 20   1 2 3 4 5 IN

Library of Congress data on file with publisher.

CONTENTS

ACKNOWLEDGEMENTS

This book has benefitted from input and constructive criticism from a number of friends. I would particularly mention Dr. Richard Hibbert; my colleagues Luc Greiner, Patrick Johnstone, and Ronaldo Lidorio; and my wife, Jean, who is always my first and last proofreader.

THE INVITATION

MUHAMMAD'S INVITATION MADE NO SENSE TO ME. Why would a man who had never introduced me to any of his own family invite the whole mission team—men, women, and children, most of whom he had never met—to his house for a midday meal? There I was, doing my best to insert myself into *his* culture without bringing *my world* with me, but he wanted to turn my approach on its head. It confused and embarrassed me.

It was only some years later that I understood. I then realised how we had mishandled that precious opportunity, and indeed many others, because we misread what was going on. I wish someone had told me how to interpret what was happening. I wish there had been a book to explain it all ahead of time. And I wish that those just starting out now on the road that I trod all those years ago had such a book to hand.

This is not that book. Not quite. This is not a collection of explanations for every possible situation that might arise, so much as a set of clues. To successfully interpret the world we find before us, we need to ask the right questions. Asking the wrong questions may yield plausible answers and even emotionally satisfying explanations, but they will also mislead us. We need to learn to observe from an informed perspective. To do that we need some pointers. An exhaustive answer-to-everything book would be unwieldy and is probably impossible. Even within such an apparently narrow field as Islam in Africa, the diversity is considerable. On top of that, we live in a time of constant change. The rising generation in Africa will bring new versions of the same challenges.

Everyone loves simple answers. The belief that there is one true method that guarantees success, that a technique is what we most need, is seductive. But it is a belief, not a fact, sustained by our cultural conditioning. You will find that this material opens up problems without offering simple solutions, but believes solutions can always be found.

In this book I attempt to prepare the Christian worker to engage fruitfully with people who identify themselves as Muslims raised in Africa. Excellent scholarly books are available to those who want to study in depth, and I shall make mention of them from time to time.

How much do we need to know about Islam or African culture to successfully introduce people to Christ? One answer would be "not much at all." At one level, we can repeat the gospel like parrots and use methods like someone following the instructions for assembling a piece of IKEA furniture. But making disciples requires two-way communication. To understand people, we need to have some idea of where they are coming from.

Furthermore, as we get to know Islam better, we also get to know the gospel better. Many workers have grown up with a thin gospel. They may be excited about it, but it is only one thread of the rich and dynamic truth that is the gospel of Christ. As we learn more about Islam, we also discover by contrast how deep and wonderful the gospel of Christ is. The same goes for culture, though this is a harder journey because it does not have the convenient theological packaging that Islam has. It requires us to reassess the very way we perceive things and to unlearn patterns we thought were simply natural.

This is a great time to be taking the gospel to African Muslims. Although all of us learn by making mistakes, my prayer is that the next generation of workers will start off with more useful knowledge than my generation did.

ISLAM PLUS AFRICA
OR
AFRICA PLUS ISLAM?

PASTOR MC CAME TO CHRIST IN A PRISON. He had been raised among the Fula people of Guinea, a people proud of their role in bringing Islam to their region. The family recognised his abilities early on and set him apart to be trained as a Muslim cleric, a "marabout." He applied himself to the arts and sciences of local Islam and also learned to support himself as a tailor in the market. Why then did this smart, hardworking young man find himself in prison in a neighbouring country? You might like to pause for a moment and think what the three most likely reasons would be. And this is not a trick question. His religious training was a factor.

No doubt many possible explanations suggest themselves, but few people guess the correct answer. First, MC was "abroad" only in the sense of living under a different secular government, but he was still very much among his own people. State borders are much less significant than ethnicity in what it means to be at home. Second, MC had been working as a sort of chaplain to a gang of thieves. His role, as a cleric, was to practice divination on behalf of the gang to determine the best and safest time to break in and steal. He provided them with Islamic charms to ward off the inevitable dangers faced by honest criminals.

One day the police raided MC's house and found stolen goods, and—long story short—he went to prison for five years. Looking back, many people ask him what he thought he was doing back then. How could a man like himself, trained in matters of religion, not know that stealing was wrong? MC shrugs and says that at the time it just seemed normal.

The important lesson we should learn from this story is not that all African Muslims are criminals or morally bankrupt. That is simply not true. The point is that our expectations mislead us. We easily assume we know how things work and how people think, and then we get surprised. The lines are drawn differently than what we would expect. If we are going to engage in transformational relationships with people, we need to understand them. To do that, we need to lay aside much of what we think we know and then commit to listening and learning.

Before we can start talking about Islam and Africa in the same sentence, we need to think about what each of those terms actually means. Islam is not just one thing. If we see it from afar, we may have a very simple idea of what we are talking about. In fact, even if we see it up close, our conditioning may deceive us into seeing less than it really is. Islam is many different things, and these things overlap to varying degrees. It is a complex reality. Our enthusiasm to simplify things for quicker understanding will not help us in the long term.

Islam is a religion, a set of beliefs and practices, and an expression of monotheism of global proportions. It is a shaper of culture, a community, and—for many—an identity. It is a way of life and a badge of honour. It is a legal and political system. It is a civilisation, rich in culture. It is a framework within which people negotiate the supernatural. It is a pathway on which people seek the true knowledge of God and of the soul. It is a patchwork of movements and associations. It is a historical reality expressed differently in different parts of the world. It is a spiritual stronghold. It is, and always has been, a political football, played with by men of power. All these descriptions are valid to some degree in any one place. Islam is many things at the same time, especially to those inside it.

It is not enough to think of Islam as a set of propositions. The core beliefs and practices are like the skeleton of a human body. On the street, you never meet skeletons; you meet living, breathing people. People do have a skeleton, but they also have muscles, fat, organs, sinews, circulation systems, skin, clothes, and—above all—life. Islam is incarnated in living communities of people, and it is with people that we deal, not with their bones.

Islam entered Africa from several different directions and in different ways. It then developed, and continues to develop, as it interacts with Africa. Many Arab and Western writers have taken Africa to be a blank canvas on which Islam, and then Christianity, came along and made their own designs. In fact, as Ghanaian missiologist John Azumah has so ably argued, Africa was and is the home of strong cultures and institutions that have shaped local expressions of both global religions.

Let's pick out some characteristics of African life that are relevant to its interaction with Islam. These are, inevitably, simple generalisations to be taken as clues to help us interpret what we find in any particular location. My only excuse in making such crude generalisations about Africans is that I shall do the same about Westerners from time to time. This is just to whet the appetite; it cannot possibly be a full analysis.

Some Characteristics of Traditional African Life

Belief in a creator God is universal. That does not mean that no African ever became an atheist, but belief in a creator God is normal. In African Traditional Religions, belief in the supreme being may not have been obvious to newly arrived missionaries, but it was present nonetheless, hidden behind a preoccupation with spirits of nature and the ancestors.

In traditional Africa, religion is inseparable from life. It is not a subject to be taught but a reality to be lived. Many African languages have no word for religion. What we have learned to distinguish as "religious matters" are, in Africa, just a normal part of the rich tapestry of existence, a set of threads that cannot be extracted from the whole. Ghanaian theologian Asamoah-

Gyadu remarks in passing that "The African context is one in which religion serves as a survival strategy."[1]

Traditionally, religious practices are tied to specific communities and locations. People live as members of families, clans, and tribes. They inhabit places fashioned by humankind in the midst of natural features such as rivers, lakes, and hills. Traditional religious practice relates to all of these. If an individual is uprooted and finds himself living in a different African community, he does not take his practices with him but rather learns to fit in to the beliefs and practices associated with the new setting.

By way of illustration, I met an evangelical pastor who, finding himself as the only non-Muslim on a long-distance bus ride, joined in the Muslim prayers. As he spoke he was experiencing a conflict. It felt like the appropriate thing to do at the time, according to his instincts, but he knew perfectly well that it was inappropriate as a Christian pastor.

It follows that religious life and identity is not first and foremost a matter of individual conviction or a personal journey of discovery. Spiritual truth and the required responses are owned by the community and are not usually subject to the personal beliefs of individuals. When different religious worlds do collide, the whole rival community is evaluated, not just a set of ideas. The most significant decisions are made by group leaders, not by the individual.

In African life, the natural and the supernatural are not separated. They occupy the same space. They are part of one reality. This is true of animistic cultures elsewhere too, of course. Ancestors are not just remembered; they are present. Customs and rituals acknowledge their presence. Such customs do not call them back from somewhere else. Visible cause and effect are real, but invisible cause and effect are also real. So if you cut down a tree in such a way that someone is unintentionally injured, the visible process is not denied, but the unseen causes are also to be investigated. Likewise, if a poorly maintained car kills a cyclist, the issues to address are not simply technical or legal.

Traditional Africa is this-worldly, or as the scholar Spencer Trimingham put it, one-worldly. The living and the dead share the same world. Life on earth is not a prelude to life in another place. This is, of course,

---

1 In Gillian Mary Bediako, Benhardt Y. Quarshie, and J. Kwabena Asamoah-Gyadu, eds., *Seeing New Facets of the Diamond: Christianity as a Universal Faith* (Eugene, OR: Wipf and Stock Publishers, 2014), 50.

in marked contrast to both Islam and Christianity. Just because a new idea is embraced, that does not mean that all related attitudes automatically realign with the new idea.

African religion is not doctrinal. It is not verbally encoded. It is not taught through distinct verbal lessons. Western-style education has only relatively recently been established in Africa. Before that, in many places, various forms of Islamic education were present too. But that does not mean that a person's basic understanding of how spiritual life works is learned or passed on through these external expressions. People learn as much, if not more, from observing as they do from what is explicitly stated. If our business is communication of a message, we should take this into account. What does this mean for discipleship? We will pick up on this topic again later on.

In Africa, religion has traditionally been non-exclusive. It is not dogmatic. It is not threatened by the presence of someone else's religious practices. It expects different ethnicities to have different practices, because religious obligations are tied to identity and not to some absolute, universal truth. Africans have no reason to prevent or to oppose alternative ways of worship unless the alternatives threaten the social order as a whole.

By the same token, African religious practice is adaptable. If circumstances change, if a proven new reality emerges, the system need not collapse. It can accommodate innovation and can adapt to a significant degree. Africans are by tradition pragmatists. They do what works.

All these things reflect underlying values in African cultures. Islam in Africa often looks and feels different than Islam in other places precisely because the underlying culture is still there. The same is true, of course, for the Arab world, the Turkic world, and so on. It follows that a standard textbook on Islam will be of limited use. Such texts enable the reader to recognise the Muslim prayers and to anticipate the major festivals, but it will not tell you what those things mean to the people who practice them in any particular place. Being acquainted with the human skeleton is not the same as understanding how a living person ticks.

TASKS, REFLECTIONS, AND MATTERS TO DISCUSS

Evaluate your pre-field preparation, and rate each on a scale from 1-10.

8

How much weight was given to methods?
To textbook Islam?
To understanding Africa?

Does the result suggest a course of action?

Additional Resources

Azumah, John A. *The Legacy of Arab-Islam in Africa*. London: Oneworld Publications, 2014.

Trimingham, J. Spencer. *The Influence of Islam upon Africa*. London: Longman, 1980.

WHAT DOES HISTORY TELL US AND WHAT DOES IT TELL THEM?

His movements were those of a man who had followed traditional routines for many years. His sitting down, his standing up, the very turn of his head, were those of an older middle-aged man: steady, unhurried, and content. It was Sunday lunch time, and I was sitting with some young men in their house. The older man had come to visit on his way home from the market. He was my host's uncle.

We chatted about where each of us was from. It seemed to me that his ethnic group and hometown did not match. He pulled out a scrap of paper and asked me to read it. It was a copy of his genealogy, going back seventeen generations. He had the original too, written on a leather scroll, but he had a paper one to carry around with him.

Something clicked. "Your ancestors rebelled against the sultan 150 years ago and were driven out, weren't they?"

"Well," he said, "the Sultan unfairly accused us—and turned against us—would be a better way of putting it. But yes, my people moved three hundred kilometres and settled there at that time."

He was pleased I knew the story. A man who carries a seventeen-generation genealogy would be.

How important is history? You don't need it to open a clinic. You don't need it to train an evangelist. You don't need it to give your testimony. But history—what is believed to have happened—is important to many, many people. There is a reason that the Bible is full of history. Oral history is maintained and valued because it contributes to identity.

Africans do not generally define themselves as individuals but as part of a group—and that group has a history: an account of the past, which may or may not be true. If you want to establish meaningful relationships with people, if you want to communicate on a deeper level, it is helpful to be aware of their history. We cannot understand how people understand themselves nor how they view the world they live in without some idea of how they see their people's story.

Knowing something of the history of Islam in Africa may also help us to understand why people are as they are and why Islam is practiced as it is. It may also be instructive about how Christianity might look in the future, because the past wields such a significant influence. Idealists may imagine that they can plant a completely new Christian movement that retains nothing of a people's past, but this is always an illusion. A people's history will throw up challenges to a new Christian movement, but it might also offer opportunities for the gospel if those opportunities are recognised.

For convenience, we can divide the history of Islam in Africa into four blocks: namely, the Swahili zone on the east coast; the Sahel along the southern borders of the Sahara; the Nilotic region, which is primarily modern Sudan; and finally, the Horn, which includes Ethiopia, Eritrea, and the Somalias. The stories of all of these have been told in overwhelming detail by J. Spencer Trimingham. Even if they are not still available in print, they are often to be found in mission libraries, collecting dust with other books left behind. Here I shall offer a mere summary of the two larger blocks and a few notes on the smaller ones.

East Africa–The Swahili Zone

The word *Swahili* comes from the Arabic word *suwaahil,* which means "coastlands." Before the emergence of Islam in Arabia, there were already Arab trading colonies down the East African coast. Among other things, these merchants traded in gold, ivory, spices, and slaves. Their enterprises were strictly coastal affairs, looking out to the wider world with no real interest in the hinterland except as a resource. They saw themselves as part of the dynamic world around the Indian Ocean, which had been a vibrant commercial zone for centuries.

The Arabs of the Swahili coast were connected to the wider Arab population and embraced Islam fairly early on, but without being hardwired into the various caliphates that arose in the Middle East or North Africa. The influences of Yemen, Egypt, and Oman were all felt at various times, but for the most part the Swahili colonies functioned as autonomous city states.

13

The Arab settlers made no attempt to conquer inland Africa nor to extend Islam into the interior. Africans became absorbed into the life of these colonies as slaves or as displaced people seeking a living. The spice trade required plantations, and the plantations needed a labour force. The descendants of the Arabs became a small elite ruling a largely African population. The various Swahili dialects—each district has its own version—combine Arabic-sourced vocabulary with Bantu linguistic patterns. In keeping with African norms, those who were absorbed into Swahili culture adopted the beliefs and practices of the people they lived with. African animist practices survived where they were useful, and the pre-Islamic Arab populations also had an animist heritage. These all fused together.

In East Africa, to be Swahili was to be Muslim—culture, identity, and community were one. To become Muslim was to become Swahili. The rural inland populations continued to follow African Traditional Religions, and the two communities lived for centuries in the same region without conflict or tension. Apart from occasional local squabbles, the Swahili communities lived and developed in peace. Islam for them was just part of the order of life.

When the Portuguese entered the Indian Ocean, they brought with them an innovation: namely, state-sponsored piracy—reinforced and justified with religious zeal. In the Indian Ocean, trading ships had not previously been armed with cannons. The Portuguese came to conquer and seize control of trade. They treated all non-Christian populations with contempt. The combination of military might, mercantile purpose, and religious identity is exemplified in the founding in 1593 of Fort Jesus in Mombasa, which stands as a powerful and visible symbol to this day. The Portuguese presence in the Swahili zone lasted about two hundred years; and following its collapse, the Sultanate of Oman exercised an elevated control in the coastal area for the following two hundred years. At one point the Oman was actually ruled from Zanzibar.

In the eighteenth and nineteenth centuries, global trade was growing rapidly. It drove the demand for all kinds of resources. The trading of slaves became industrial in scale, and the Swahili communities started to push inland to access greater resources. Some inland ethnic groups became "client peoples," reorganising their way of life around the Swahili traders, depending on their protection and benefitting from their resources. In due course they adopted Islamic identity. Then, after a brief competition between Britain and Germany, British rule was established over most of the Swahili zone. This had the effect of accelerating the spread of Islam inland. The British encouraged the wider use of the Swahili language and the movement of people outside of their usual homelands. The alien nature of the British administration posed challenges to traditional rural life through the establishment of schools. The creation of new administrative entities put distinct peoples under one roof in unfamiliar ways, running counter to traditional patterns. And, as we know, the British presence also allowed Christianity to enter the interior.

All these developments tended to undermine traditional culture and work against tribal living patterns. It gave value to having a global (rather than strictly local) identity, a factor which helped both Islam and Christianity. Islam had the advantage of already being Africanised. In the areas recently afflicted by slave raiding, Christianity had the advantage of being associated with deliverance and the imposition of a new peaceful order. British rule also brought an influx of Asian Muslims, among them Shi'ites and Ahmadis, but their impact on East African Islam has been minimal so far.

West Africa–The Sahel

The experience of West Africa was quite different, but first there is a curious commonality. The word *Sahel* also comes from Arabic and also means "coast." The consonants *s*, *h*, and *l* occur in both words, and *suwaahil* is the plural of *saahil*. The Sahel refers to the area that runs along the southern edge of the Sahara. For traders, crossing the desert was much like crossing the sea. The Sahara, like the ocean, was dangerous. If you navigated badly, death was the likely result. In the Sahara, just as at sea, drinking water was a scarce commodity. An oasis in the desert functioned as an island did for ocean voyages. Prolonged sand storms posed a serious threat to survival.

No one attempted the crossing without a good reason, and to do so successfully required skill and courage. The "ship" used to cross the dry expanse was the camel—or more accurately, the camel train. The popular description of the camel as "the ship of the desert" is actually a translation of the Arabic *safiinat al-Sahara*. Crossing the Sahara was a logistical challenge every bit as great as crossing an ocean. What was the attraction? Why do it?

In medieval times, there was a succession of major African states based on rivers and extending over very large areas. Some of their names, confusingly, were later adopted by countries whose territories were elsewhere: Ghana, Mali, Songhai, and Kanem. Their locations and histories can easily be found online. These states functioned quite differently than those of Europe (as explained in detail by Trimingham), but nevertheless were powerful kingdoms. They were able to provide safe access to gold, ivory, ebony, and slaves.

It would be a mistake to assume that obvious outsiders could travel freely in the medieval African world. The presence of the African states provided the stability and necessary protection that allowed foreign traders to operate. From the traders, African rulers bought cloth and high-quality metal goods. The connection with Mediterranean Africa brought immense wealth to these states and gave them access to the wider world.

The traders started coming in the tenth century from what is now Morocco. Under the protection of the African states, they formed privileged enclaves and ran their own affairs. That a foreign people had their own religious customs was to be expected in African thinking. The African royal clans, along with their entourages, added Islamic identity to their traditional civic and cultic functions and adopted the Muslim prayers. They did not adopt the civil, social, or family law of Islam, nor did they seek to Islamise their populations. They did adopt the practice of pilgrimage to Mecca, displaying extraordinary wealth to the wondering masses as they made their way across the Muslim world. Their Islam had more to do with prestige and privilege than submission. Ibn Battuta, the fourteenth-century Moroccan traveller and writer, was both impressed and horrified at what he found when he visited the legendary kingdom of Mali.[2]

With the passage of time, small Berber populations from Morocco and Mauritania settled in the Sahel and set up within it east-west trading networks, in addition to the trans-Saharan routes. The Berber traders married African wives and created client peoples. Africans who were detribalised through war or slavery were absorbed into their network. Just as the East African Swahili colonies had a distinctive culture, so the trading peoples of West Africa had one too. In some local African languages, the word *trader* was shorthand for *Muslim.* At some point, the nomadic peoples— by definition, those least attached to place and time—also adopted Islam as suitable for their way of life and for the alliances that they made. The traders lived and worked in peace under the protection of the nominally Muslim African states. The traders were themselves client peoples.

However, there was also a major difference between the Sahel and the Swahili. The Berber peoples of the west only fully adopted Islam when they had developed their own version of it with their own leaders. They established Sufi-style relational structures, in which a teacher would train up his own family and all those who came under his roof. These people could teach Islam, provide Islamic folk remedies, travel, and trade. Trimingham dubs these "clerical clans."

Authority was derived from the head of the order in one specific locality, but the body of practitioners were highly mobile. This class of religious practitioners spread with and through the trader and nomad networks, giving substance to Islam as a physical presence among ordinary people and providing spiritual services. These Muslim clerics introduced literacy to the African states. The kings retained a small body of Muslim scribes and advisors. The majority population—the farmers, fishermen, and hunters— continued in their traditional ways. They were not at all threatened by the fact that people of a different lifestyle practiced a different religion, nor that from them they could buy spiritual services as they had need.

2 Ibn Battuta, *Travels in Asia and Africa 1325-1354* (London: Routledge & Kegan Paul, 1984 reprint), chapter XIV.

About 1600, there was a major change. The Kingdom of Morocco conquered the Sahelian state of Songhai. Although the Moroccans won the battle, their rule of the African kingdom disintegrated within a generation or two, and with it the order that had prevailed up until then. A time of great instability followed, in which smaller states—some led by rulers claiming Islamic identity and some who did not—rose and fell. According to Trimingham, some states entered Islam in one generation and then left it in the next. This instability led to more armed conflict, which in turn broke up stable communities. Detribalised people tended to attach themselves to Islam, which provided a pattern of life not primarily determined by ancestry and location. Firearms became more common. And at least in part in response to the growing global market, private armies emerged and engaged in aggressive slave raiding. While the disorder contributed to the flow of local people into Islam, the animosity also hardened the attitude of others against Islam.

In this period, Islam itself frequently became part of the conflict between states. Jihads were declared. Uthman dan Fodio (1754–1817), in what is now Nigeria, and Umar Taal (1794–1864), in the Guinea-Senegal area, were the two most significant leaders of jihad. Although both were ethnic Fulanis, they were associated with different Sufi brotherhoods. The justification given for jihad was to force Muslims to implement shari'a—that is to say, the civil and family law normally disregarded in Africa. However, whatever idealism may have inspired the preachers soon evaporated and was replaced by general opportunism and tyranny.

17

The penetration of the British and French into the region in the nineteenth century imposed a new order, welcomed by many and resented by others. The Europeans arrived with little understanding of African institutions, but with some previous experience of dealing with Muslim governments. Consequently, they affirmed Islamic rulers even in areas that had only recently come under Muslim rule and whose population did not wholeheartedly accept it. In so doing, they strengthened the hold of Muslim culture as against traditional ways.

As in the Swahili zone, the changes brought by European government did much to accelerate Islamisation. The peace enabled trade to flourish. The creation of new political territories led to the greater circulation of persons of influence. Trade languages were preferred over local languages. Schooling and Christian missions challenged the norms of traditional African living. All these things contributed to making African Islam an attractive and necessary identity in those areas where it was already present.

Sudan and the Horn

The experiences of Sudan and the Horn (the area around Ethiopia) were significantly different from the Swahili and the Sahel in that they both had Christian states in place before the arrival of Islam. In the case of Sudan, centuries of pressure, conflict, and natural decay brought about the demise of the Christian kingdoms. In addition, unlike the rest of Africa, the proximity of Egypt and the Arabian Peninsula allowed a much greater penetration of the Arabs and their culture into what is now Sudan. Unlike other sub-Saharan countries, the Arabic language took root, allowing Arab culture to significantly rewrite the DNA of the communities there. Nevertheless, local pre-Islamic traditions and ethnic identities live on, especially in the outlying areas furthest from the Nile Valley. In the late twentieth century and early twenty-first century the Arabisation of Sudan intensified and the pre-Islamic ethnic identities strengthened in reaction to it. This was one of the active elements in the political crisis of 2019.

The Christian state of Ethiopia survived centuries of coexistence with Islam. The history of the Horn—which, of course, includes the Somali people among others—is complex and quite different from that of the other regions of Africa, and this is not the place for a detailed and specialist exposition.

Some Historical Legacies

Identity usually draws on history. There are peoples in Africa for whom the memory of Islam as the religion of predatory slave raiders still looms large. Some nurture a victim status, a reason to define themselves as non-Muslim, and this inhibits the spread of Islam as a community. Likewise, there are many for whom Christianity is so closely associated with alien invasion from Europe that to even consider the religion is a betrayal of their heritage. This may be particularly true for Muslim peoples.

If you want to really become acquainted with a people, explore their history from their point of view. How do they see themselves? Are they a dominant people for whom Islamic identity is part of their right to rule? Are they a downtrodden people for whom Islam was something imposed by others? It may be that they accept Islam because there is no practical alternative; and so, on that basis, it must be the true religion even though it is also associated in their mind with their subject status and with oppression. This factor has been significant in the strong response to the gospel among some North African Berbers.

The important thing is not what textbooks say about history, but how history is received. It is useful to be aware of the more formal version of history to get a framework of understanding, but we should not make the mistake of trying to teach Africans their own history. Rather, we should listen and seek to understand what they have been told and what it signifies to them. We may need to learn how to ask helpful questions. In the West we are taught to ask direct questions and to expect factual answers. This is not normal behaviour in many cultures. Asking questions is a relational exercise. How a person answers depends on the relationship. If the answer comes in the form of a story, it may take some reflection before we find what we are looking for.

Westerners, owing to the experience we have gained from our own cultures, tend to assume that people change religious identity (i.e., convert) as a result of deep, individual conviction. We also often assume that the use of one's mother tongue is critical and so make literacy central to spiritual life. History demonstrates that Islam successfully transplanted itself into Africa without such a conviction and without investing in indigenous languages. Before we protest that we would not want to take lessons from Islam, we should consider what our own assumptions about conversion through individual conviction are based upon. In a later chapter we shall look at individualism more fully.

19

In the past, detribalised people were absorbed into Islam, and today some detribalised people find a home in church communities. Alongside this were villages, clans, and tribes that moved *en bloc* into Islam. Likewise, there have also been occasions when whole villages or tribes have embraced Christianity. Because we read the Scriptures through the lenses of individualism, we miss the examples of group dynamics in the New Testament. In Acts 16 we read of two households—and a household included servants as well as the nuclear family—who were baptised together. In Samaria, Stephen's preaching and miracles produced a mass movement. So did Paul's ministry in Ephesus. To be sure, something was happening at the individual level, but there was also a collective shift. In many cultures, major decisions are not made by the individual, and especially not by young individuals, but by the group leadership.

Today and Tomorrow

A man in his thirties who belonged to an ethnic group that was proud of its Islamic credentials made a decision. After a long period of searching, he became a Christian. His father was dead. He went and told his mother. She listened carefully and told him that if he must be a Christian, he should be a good one, and that she was just glad that he was not joining Boko Haram. He went to his personal friend, the town governor, and got much the same response.

I was riding in a bush taxi a few years ago. In one corner of the windshield was a sticker with a portrait of Bin Laden. This was while Bin Laden was still in hiding. I turned to the driver, pointed to the picture, and asked, "Friend of yours?"

"This car does not belong to me," he said. "And that man has caused us nothing but trouble."

History is made up of yesterday's current affairs. African Muslims often take much more interest in international current affairs than do people in our home communities. They relate what is going on in the wider world to what is going on in their own local setting. The high-profile "war on terror" which sets the West (still associated with Christianity) against militant Islamic movements splits African sympathies, especially when the conflict is played out on African soil. Islamic militants draw on deeply felt ethnic grievances, but they also alienate many others for whom harmony is the highest priority.

Developments on the world stage while you are living in Africa will affect who people think you are. They will also influence what they think the gospel is about. More accurately, it is their perception of world events—the way their community processes them—that has an important influence. While we might feel an inner imperative to have them listen to our own take on what is relevant and even what we believe to be true about these things, we need to be ready to hear what they are saying and to understand it. These things may well play into how people understand what we are doing and why.

TASKS, REFLECTIONS, AND MATTERS TO DISCUSS

Find out how the people you are working among see themselves in relation to other peoples. Do they see themselves as rulers or subjects? Bear in mind that getting good answers may depend on whether you are trusted. You need a good relationship to get good communication. People do not necessarily share knowledge freely. Bear in mind that a matter is confirmed by two or three witnesses.

21

Find out what part Islam plays in history from their point of view. Do old people and young people tell the same story?

Look for aspects of their pre-Islamic past/culture of which they are proud. In some cases, it is possible that they do not recognise these things as non-Islamic if they have been fully absorbed into their Islamicised culture.

 Listen to what they are saying to each other about global trends. Which international stories matter to them? What does this imply?

Is there any tension between their ethnic heritage and their Islamic identity? Discuss with team members what this might mean for the gospel.

Additional Resources

Azumah, John A. *The Legacy of Arab-Islam in Africa.* London: Oneworld Publications, 2014.

Battuta, Ibn. *Travels in Asia and Africa 1325–1354.* London: Routledge & Kegan Paul, 1984.

Cornelius, Charles. *A History of the East African Coast.* Kindle, 2015.

Fleming, Fergus. *The Sword and the Cross.* London: Faber & Faber, 2004.

Injeeli, Akhtar. *Sufism and Jihad.* Chapter 6. CGE Publishing, 2012.

Trimingham, J. Spencer. *A History of Islam in West Africa.* Oxford: Oxford Paperbacks, 1970.

———. *Islam in East Africa.* Oxford: Clarendon, 1964.

———. *Islam in Ethiopia.* London: Routledge, 2007.

———. *Islam in the Sudan.* London: Routledge, 1965.

For a quick introduction to the great medieval states of West Africa, see: http://www.bbc.co.uk/worldservice/africa/features/storyofafrica/index_section4.shtml.

THE AFRICAN
INCARNATION
OF ISLAM

A crowd formed around a Western missionary woman laying out a stall of Christian books, DVDs, and SIM cards in a nomad cattle market. A young Muslim teacher approached her and demanded that she remove herself and her wares. She retorted, "I believe in God, I pray, I fast—What's your problem?"

The crowd sided with the missionary, and the teacher was silenced. But he stayed. He read. He took. He distributed media clips to his friends.

In Africa, the practices of Islam are primary. Charles Marsh, who worked for many years in Algeria before moving to Chad in the 1960s, was not the first to observe that African Muslims are much more observant of the prayers than those in the Maghreb. A Jordanian might pride himself on being a good Muslim but still only pray two or three times in any given day. In Africa, the prayers are paramount. In Chad, the shorthand description Muslims use to describe themselves is "those who pray and fast," rather than those who confess Muhammad, read the Qur'an, follow shari'a, or any other description people might use elsewhere. This seems to be true generally in Africa. It resonates with the underlying African approach to religious life.

The prayers are the daily mark of Muslim affiliation, and Ramadan is the annual equivalent. The month of fasting is a much greater expression of community than the prayers can ever be because the whole household is necessarily involved. I have met proud Turkish Muslims who have never fasted more than a few days, but in Africa Ramadan is not optional. Even those who are technically exempt often still participate. The whole community is reorganised into the new rhythm.

I spoke to a man at the height of an extremely hot Ramadan and asked him how it was going. "I love it," he beamed. "It is the best time of year."

"Then why don't you continue for an extra month or two?" I asked.

His face fell. "What? On my own? Of course not. That would be impossible."

Ramadan is a collective community experience. And it is not particularly spiritual in the narrow Western sense of the word—that is, being primarily an internal matter.

Not everyone finds Ramadan to be sweetness and light. My friend was making lots of money from it. For others, it is a time of great hardship. The level of anger, arguments, and domestic conflict often rises noticeably, especially in the first ten days or so, but still the community side is highly valued. Those who cheat don't admit it. The month of fasting is held in high honour.

By contrast, those dimensions of Islam consisting of law, doctrine, and philosophy have little place. The *shahada,* the confession of faith in God and his messenger, and the *iman,* the core beliefs, are affirmed because that is what you do if you are a Muslim. It is an issue of external behaviour rather than of personal conviction.

That does not mean that personal conviction is absent or that people are secretly riddled with doubt. No, personal conviction is settled by the imperative of conforming to the community. Neither personal doubt nor personal belief are major factors. Belief is an act of obedience, just like Islamic prayer. In the same way that you don't have to understand the Arabic words for your prayers to be valid, so you don't need to have explored the meaning of the *shahada* and personally taken ownership of it for your faith to be valid. Preaching in the mosque focuses on behaviour, not beliefs. Confessing the oneness of God is a practice, not a mystery to explore.

While African Islam is primarily about the daily practices required by the faith, Islam as a comprehensive system of civil law has never taken root. The jihads of the eighteenth and nineteenth centuries were unleashed by scholars who lamented the lack of Islamic civil life, but their reforms lasted only a brief time before more relational and traditional practices reasserted themselves. Simple things like marriage and divorce are broadly compliant with shari'a, but the intricacies of inheritance law, which fill the tomes of Islamic jurists, are largely ignored. As a rule, practicing Islam under a state-run, secular legal code is not a great stress point for African Muslims.

As a general rule, Muslim identity is tied to ethnic identity. The observance of Islamic ritual does not make a person a Muslim, and failure to do so does not nullify Islamic identity; rather, performing the rituals is the approved expression of that identity. There are exceptions to the close tie between ethnicity and religious affiliation. In parts of East Africa and in southwestern Nigeria, for example, people of the same ethnicity may have different religious affiliations. But in most areas, if you know a person's ethnicity, you know what religion he or she belongs to. The underlying cultural pattern of religious practice being tied to ethnicity and place reinforces that tendency.

Other cultural patterns, such as preferring the group over the individual and the pragmatic accommodation to power, also reinforce the tendency to tie religious allegiance to ethnic identity. (We will further explore these issues later.) The upshot is that when people turn to Christ, they are more likely to be asked why they have betrayed their ancestors than why they have not remained true to Muhammad.

In Africa, religion is woven into life. It is not a thing to be thought of separately from everyday interactions. The community dimension of Islam is well adapted to this approach. Just as ethnicity is a matter of public knowledge, so is religion. The two go together as identity markers. The idea of religious belief and practice as things distinct from the rest of life, and especially of them being a matter of personal choice, is primarily a recent and Western cultural approach. The African way has more in common with the rest of the world, and in that sense needs no special explanation.

Blood sacrifice is common across much of Muslim Africa. The slaughter of animals often accompanies rites of passage such as baby naming, circumcision, marriage, and death. Sacrifices are integral to making the rite a community event. However, when sacrifices are made ahead of sowing the fields or harvesting, clearly something more than the celebration of community is occurring. If you ask people why they make sacrifices or how it fits within Islam, you will find that they don't know. Those are not questions that they ask. They just know that is important to do it. Sacrifices are not made to a named spirit, nor are they overtly made to God, as in the Old Testament; but the requirements of Islamic slaughter practices give the sacrifice an Islamic feel. The manner of slaughter is Islamic, but the underlying purpose of the sacrifice is pre-Islamic.

In Africa, Sufism has led the way. In some parts of the world, Sufism developed alongside and even in conflict with systems of government whose legal machinery was based on Islam. Such was not generally the case south of the Sahara. Islam was introduced and modelled by traders influenced by Sufi approaches, and it has been Sufi-style Islam that has penetrated the lives of ordinary people. The problem with making such a statement, however, is that Sufism is as diverse as Islam itself. Sufism in Turkey and Iran has great poetic traditions. India has developed pantheistic forms. Some forms of Sufism are pacifist, while others are militaristic. As with other aspects of Islam, we should not assume that what we know of Sufism elsewhere will be replicated in Africa.

Before we look at Sufism in Africa, we need to sketch a basic outline of what we mean by Sufism in general. Sufis see Muhammad as the perfect man, a man who not only believed and practiced religion correctly but also had a pious, seeking heart that sought connection with God. He meditated. He sought and received experiences of God. Generally speaking, Sufi groups believe that in addition to the formal set of beliefs and practices passed down to all Muslims, a secret oral tradition was revealed to those who showed themselves worthy. Such knowledge included deeper interpretations of the Qur'an.

All forms of Sufism honour the Qur'an, the Hadith, and the sharia, but many allow authorities other than the scholars to speak. In some streams, sheikhs may pass on secret traditions; in others, the sheikhs claim to have attained such a closeness to God that they can give fresh interpretations. Some are commissioned, through visions by Muhammad or other great men of the past, to renew Islam. Sufism allows access to fresh divine authority that does not require years of dry scholarship. While history is still honoured, the holy men of the past inhabit the present through the sheikh.

Sufism also tends to be relational in its organisation. Sufis practice discipleship in ways similar to those we find in the Gospels. A serious seeker commits to learning from a master to whom he submits, along with other seekers. The relationship is with the master, not the book or the system. The master transmits methods as well as information. In fact, knowledge is mainly transmitted through practices to be imitated, and only later understood, and may never be explained verbally.

Sufi-style Islam allows living humans to interpret the changing world with fresh insights. Sufi masters have found their own ways of accommodating the religious sympathies and aspirations of non-Muslim host cultures across Asia and in Africa. From one point of view, they make syncretism possible under a cloak of Islamic respectability. From another, they build bridges that enable people to enter into Islam and adopt an Islamic identity without completely leaving their culture behind.

29

Many forms of Sufism not only revere living sheikhs as saints but also turn their tombs into sacred sites. It works like this. Those who get close to God get *baraka,* which is usually translated as "blessing," though that is too narrow of a translation. It is divinely derived, impersonal power. The baraka remains in their family and at their tomb, enabling the emergence of special sites where access to unseen power is available. Believers seek closeness to God and supernatural intervention in their lives by going to the tombs of the saints. Since Sufi saints are channels of divine power, people go to them for healing, good luck, fortune-telling, protection from evil, and so on. Those who peddle charms and other artefacts do so within a Sufi-influenced tradition.

Researchers who try to measure the presence of Sufism meet a difficulty. The number of living Sufi masters is always quite small. The number of dedicated disciples (usually called *mureed*s) is also limited. Does that mean that Sufism is a minority activity? Not at all, because the population as a whole believes in the forms of Sufism it knows. The mass of ordinary people—including chiefs and officials—consult Sufi practitioners as they have need. So Sufism as a discipline is limited in Africa, but as an influence it is all-pervasive. Elsewhere in the world, the word *faqiih* means an expert in Islamic law and *faqiir* means an expert in mystical Islamic spirituality. In much of Africa, the two are merged into one—that is to say, the Sufi-style cleric is also considered the main access to Islamic law.

Some international expressions of Sufism are either unknown or extremely rare in African Islam. Whirling dervishes, for example, are present in Sudan but not elsewhere. The wandering hermit-style Sufis, often called Qalandars, are absent from most of Africa. Major tomb cults are found in Senegal, Mali, Sudan, and the Horn, but not in most of West and Central Africa. The Comoro Islands have them, and East Asians have introduced them into some parts of East Africa.

The influence of Sufism on how people think extends way beyond tomb cults. Consider this story told by Rudiger Seesemann on page six of his book *The Divine Flood.*

> On his way home from the market, a man carrying a bag full of meat passed by the mosque of Medina. As it was the time of the congregational prayer, he stopped and entered the mosque. Fearing that someone might steal the meat if he left it at the entrance, he took the bag inside and placed it next to his feet. Baye was leading the prayer, and after it was over, the man went home to prepare his meal. But to his great amazement, the meat remained raw; in fact, it did not change its consistency at all, as if it was not on the fire. Disturbed by this experience, he went to inform Baye about the incident. Baye listened patiently and responded: "Everything that is behind me in congregational prayer is immune against fire."

The word *Baye* is a Wolof word meaning "father," here a term of respect referring to Sheikh Ibrahim Niasse (spelling varies); and Medina, in this case, is the settlement in Senegal founded by the sheikh. Niasse (1900–75) was the most important sheikh in the Tijani Sufi order in the twentieth century. His portrait appears on stickers in taxi windshields and on posters in neighbourhood shops across Africa. Although Niasse was a reputable scholar of Islam, he is most widely known and revered as a saint of great spiritual power. His movement, the "Divine Flood," made Tijani Sufism a truly mass movement across much of Africa, displacing other orders, such as the Qadiriya. If you google his name, you will find the same images that appear in the stores found on almost every street corner. To this day, reports about him appearing to people in Nigeria cause great excitement.

While in principle such Sufi sheikhs always direct people to the example of Muhammad and to the worship God, the sheikhs themselves occupy a highly treasured place in the hearts of the people. It is sometimes said that Islam offers religion but not a saviour. Men like Niasse come very close to being saviour-type figures.

Clearly the fact that Sufis operate in an open spiritual world, in which visible and invisible realms coexist, resonates well with the underlying African approach to the supernatural. Similarly, the highly relational organisation and expression of community adapt well. The hands-on, concrete approach to the transmission of religious practice commends itself to Africa. While the approach of law-based Islam elsewhere in the world cannot easily tolerate deviation, Sufism is relaxed about a variety of practices and beliefs being side by side within a town or community. Sufi clerics respond to those who seek them out. They don't (usually) impose their ways on the resistant. All these things, along with the inherent adaptability of Sufism, makes it a "good fit" for Africa, and almost all of African Islam exhibits a Sufi influence.

Just as the external duties of Islam, such as the prayers and the fasting, are primary in Africa, so is the most obvious manifestation of Sufism, which is *zikir*. The term *zikir* (literally "remembrance") refers to the practice of chanting over and over again the confession of faith, or the names of God, or some other Qur'anic text. At set times, men meet with their local sheikh and chant. In classical Sufism, chanting is a key tool in advancing in the knowledge of God. In Africa, the aspirations may be lower: perhaps the hope of a touch from the invisible world. The practice is all the more noticeable, as participants frequently use PA systems that broadcast their chanting. Prolonged chanting or recitations at night to commemorate the departed also contribute to the soundscape of many neighbourhoods.

The practice of following the official prayers by remembering the names of God, using prayer beads, is also a common Sufi practice. Different Sufi movements have their own version of the prayer beads.

Within Africa, we also find local Sufi movements. One of the best known is that of the Muridiya of Amadou Bamba in Senegal, which played a key role in bringing the Wolof people into Islam and resisting French rule.

It is not true, as some have claimed, that Islam is a superficial veneer spread over African animism. Islam has made itself at home in Africa and, as it were, married into the community. It has adapted and belongs. It is felt to be as much a part of African life as anything else. In well-established Muslim communities, Islam is as deeply woven into identity as ethnicity and language. Just as in the traditional ways of Africa religion is woven into life as it is lived and not perceived as some separate element, so Islam is woven into the lives of those raised in it.

This kind of Islam is deeply resistant to the gospel. The attachment to Islam is not in that part of a person's world or of a community's life in which choices are made. To oppose Islam and its practices is to set oneself against one's family, one's people, and against life itself. In such a setting, people can admire Christianity without ever recognising its call on their lives.

As a general rule, African Muslims are resistant to the gospel without being hostile to Christians. Diversity is accepted as a normal reality in their world. The fact that others follow a different religion does not in itself pose any challenge or threat. In general, Muslims and Christians can live alongside each other in peace. Of course, where conversions are taking place, tensions and conflict may break out; but such tensions arise from the strain on community relations and the threat to local social order, not from the implacability of two opposing systems. Although persecution happens—and Scripture tells us that it is normal—the power of kinship is strong. More often than not, in the long run, reconciliation is possible.

TASKS, REFLECTIONS, AND MATTERS TO DISCUSS

Find out from local people what identifies someone as "a man of God."

If outward actions demonstrate religious allegiance, how should followers of Christ behave? Does the teaching of Jesus support secret allegiance? If not, what actions or behaviour should characterise his followers? Is it necessary for such patterns of behaviour to contrast with those of Muslims on all points?

Where religious belief and practice are so closely woven into identity and culture, can Christ be taken into the life of the community, or must believers be extracted?

Write a summary of the gospel message that you want to communicate. Then reread this chapter asking yourself how it might sound to the hearer. What would come across as utterly foreign? What would be welcome? If you have a trusted local friend, present your written message as something that others say and ask him or her what they make of it.

Are there elements of Sufi practice that can be harnessed for the gospel?

To what extent should new believers participate in the rites of passage of their non-Christian neighbours?

Additional Resources

Hadaway, Robin Dale. "Magical Mystical Muslims: Sufi-Oriented Islam and African Traditional Religion." In *Margins of Islam: Ministry in Diverse Muslim Contexts*, edited by Gene Daniels and Warrick Farah. Pasadena, CA: William Carey Publishing, 2018.

Seesemann, Rudiger. *The Divine Flood: Ibrahim Niasse and the Roots of a Twentieth-Century Sufi Revival*. Oxford: Oxford University Press, 2011.

Trimingham, J. Spencer. *The Sufi Orders in Islam*. Oxford: Oxford University Press, 1971.

"OF COURSE, THERE AREN'T ANY *REAL* MUSLIMS HERE."

The title of this chapter is a remark I have heard several times from workers in different West African countries. What does it mean, and is it in any way true?

It means that the Islam found in a particular place does not match the Islam described in textbooks. It is a feature of Western thought that we tend to regard the official version of Islam as a true and accurate representation and then judge what we find accordingly. In doing so, we inadvertently align ourselves with the Islamic radicals.

Who decided that Islam was not permitted to change and develop over time in different locations? Textbook Islam does not exist as a living reality anywhere in the world. How then can it be real? Before we get too philosophical about this, let us just agree to accept that if a community describes itself as Muslim, then it has the right to do so. It is not for us to say or even think that they ought to be practicing Islam differently.

One thing that causes people to say that a local expression of Islam is not real Islam is the presence of what are called "folk practices." A number of writers have very helpfully described the many practices that do not originate from the founding of Islam but which are widespread among Muslim communities (see below). Such writers also demonstrate that the values that many ordinary people assign to the standard Islamic rituals do not correspond with the teaching of Islamic scholars. This all gets lumped under the general heading of "folk Islam" and is then treated as something apart, not really Islam.

This approach misses the point. There have always been beliefs and practices among Muslims in every part of the world that do not stem from the Qur'an or from the example of Muhammad. The fact that many African beliefs and practices survive or were adapted after the advent of Islam should not distract us. For those raised in these environments, it is all Islam, with the sanction of God Almighty behind it. We need to relate to them as they are, not how we were misled to believe they should be.

Along with the idea that textbook Islam is real comes an approach that assumes that Muslims are to be addressed along the lines of doctrine. "You believe X. X is not true. Y is the truth." This approach is becoming less common. It is largely ineffective because African Muslims do not learn Islam as a set of propositions. They learn what to do and what to say as a matter of practice. They may or may not learn the reasoning behind it all. Their attachment to Islam is not generally due to their believing it to be true. They believe it is true because that is what is required of Muslims. It would be improper to disbelieve the religion of your forefathers. Belonging comes first, behaving comes next, and believing follows along somewhere behind, if at all.

If outsiders come along, explicitly setting themselves against Islam, then no matter how coherent, or indeed true, their words are, they will be seen as hostile—not people of peace, not people to be taken seriously. An East African proverb states, "I cannot hear the words you are saying for the thunder of what you are." In keeping with so many cultural values, the choice of who a person should listen to and who to trust is determined by who the speaker is and how they are connected to the listener—not by the power of their argument. To put it another way, trust comes from relationship. Like the sheep in John 10, they will not follow a stranger. Where there is no relationship, behaviour determines whether or not a speaker is credible. Being right in what we say is not enough.

As we have intimated, in Africa religion is traditionally not a separate department of life, nor is the invisible world—what we refer to as the supernatural—separated. The assumption is that those who speak for God also know how to navigate the invisible. To put it another way, those who are found to be able to negotiate with the invisible world are people who can be trusted in matters pertaining to God.

To make a sweeping generalisation, Africans tend to be pragmatic rather than dogmatic. Islam has established its credibility more through its "folk practices" than any theological debate. It is also not unknown for Christian workers to see breakthroughs in a community as a result of some very clear demonstration of spiritual power. Islamic folk practices, far from being some sort of extra baggage cluttering "true Islam," are the key which has enabled Islam to penetrate to the level of ordinary people and to maintain its place in their lives. If Christians assume that the arrival of the gospel will lead to a rapid shift toward Western ways of thinking, they are sadly mistaken. The implications for the gospel are huge.

Christian anthropologist Paul Hiebert popularised the idea of the "excluded middle." He argues that the Western missionary movement has been effective on two levels but failed on the third. At the "top" level, concerning matters such as the remedies for eternity, the nature of God, reconciliation with God, and so on, missions have successfully imparted teaching which has taken root and is being transmitted within the new Christian communities. On the practical, earthly level, the Christian movement has made available, and continues to make available, Western science-based medicine, along with technical benefits in agriculture, machinery, and technology—all supported by an education system. Between the heavenly and earthly levels lies a middle zone, that which deals with the invisible world—the hidden causes and effects.

In Africa, as in many other parts of the world, there is a keen awareness of the invisible world, and if Christian movements ignore it or dismiss it, people will inevitably look to others who can help with such matters. In many churches in West Africa, pastors exhort their congregations not to go to the marabout but to entrust their loved ones to the church-run clinic or even the state health system. However, as long as the perception is that many underlying causes are not addressed through modern medicine, the marabouts will find customers. Their activities include operating in Hiebert's excluded middle, which is being denied or ignored by Christian institutions even though it is a living reality in the lives of ordinary people.

It is not that everything people believe is true, but rather that they need practitioners who exercise discernment and can plausibly interpret what is happening to them. These matters were alive in Bible times. In Scripture, the gospel addressed them in both theory and practice.

What do Muslim practitioners do? In any particular locality, you can expect to find a whole range of practices, identified locally as part of Islam, for dealing with the invisible world. People go to a cleric, who might be called a *sheikh, marabout,* or *faqeer,* to get diagnoses for illness or infertility and to explain misfortune. They obtain remedies for afflictions and protections from evil. For example, the ink used for writing the Qur'an on wooden slates is washed off and dispensed as liquid power. Specific verses may be written out, washed off, and then drunk by the sufferer or smeared on the body. A practitioner might take the ink in his own mouth and spit it at the patient.

There is a whole occult science of charm writing. Those who have been instructed in this secret knowledge believe certain passages of the Qur'an have special properties. These are written out and packed into small leather charms to be worn on the body, placed in a home, or attached to an animal. Some charms draw on formulas that are not based on the Qur'an at all but are passed on from master to disciple.

Practitioners may prescribe sacrifices, chanting, or pilgrimages, but what they all have in common is that consultations require some kind of payment. I asked Pastor MC, whose story is told in chapter 2, what happened if people did not get the help/protection/cure they were paying for. He said that they were told that someone else was using something against them which was more powerful and, of course, more expensive.

The role once played by the witchdoctor or shaman is now played by the marabout. The cleric is not just a source of information about ancient doctrines rooted in Arab history. He is connected with the powers of the invisible world and authorised by God. African tradition takes the invisible world seriously, and African Islam provides approved ways of interacting with it.

The New Testament shows us the apostles, and indeed others (Philip, for example), applying the gospel to the unseen world. Paul taught in Ephesians and Colossians that all invisible powers are defeated and subject to Christ. Paul taught that gifts of knowledge and wisdom were made available within a church by the Holy Spirit (1 Cor 12). Acts 2 indicates that the Holy Spirit, who previously only operated through the prophets, was now released into the whole people of God.

In Old Testament times, the prophets did not just foretell the coming of Christ or deliver messages about repentance; they were available to the people to consult over things going on in their lives (e.g., 1 Sam 9:9; 2 Kgs 1:6; 3:11–19). The same passage in Deuteronomy 18 that forbids occult practices (verses 9–13) also promises the ministry of the prophet, the one who speaks for God (verses 14–22). The thing that was forbidden was not seeking information about the invisible world, but rather seeking such information apart from God.

This doesn't mean the only style of ministry that can be effective is one of signs and wonders, but it does mean that all Christian workers should take the supernatural seriously. Learning to hear God is just as important as any practical skill. Maintaining closeness to God is as vital as language learning. Recognising gifts within a team is vital. Discipling Jesus-style should include teaching by word and deed on how to deal with the invisible world. The great Christian distinctive in this area is what Jesus himself taught. "Freely you have received; freely give" (Matt 10:8). The name of Christ is to be used without charge.

One day I was leading a new believer through a Bible study and we were reading the passage in Genesis 40 about Joseph in prison. The other prisoners were disturbed by their dreams, so Joseph invited them to share what they had seen and expressed confidence that God would give the interpretation. Inevitably, my friend looked up at me and said, "I had a dream." My heart sank. I had never done any dream interpretation before. But I affirmed my trust in God and asked him to tell me his dream. I was able to interpret it, and what I said came to pass.

It is not a matter of recklessly launching out and pretending to be something we are not; it is a matter of walking with the Lord and trusting him to work through us.

If we are to have credibility as servants of God, we need to be known to be able to deal with the invisible world. Furthermore, our disciples will need to be equipped to operate in this area with confidence, as followers of Christ. It is in just this environment that they will be following Christ.

TASKS, REFLECTIONS, AND MATTERS TO DISCUSS

 Find out what kind of issues people take to Muslim practitioners. Observe where charms are placed, and if you can ask in a nonthreatening way, find out what these charms are expected to accomplish.

 On what basis do people choose which practitioners to go to? Kinship? Expertise? Cost?

Read Acts looking for indications of how people then were relating to the invisible world, and observe how the apostles responded.

On a scale of 1 to 10, how ready are you to deal with
1) discerning the voice of God for someone?
2) praying for healing?
3) praying for deliverance from evil powers?
How might a person become more ready?

Find out how significant power encounters have been in the lives of those who are already believers.

Additional Resources

Hiebert, Paul. *Anthropological Insights for Missionaries*. Grand Rapids: Baker, 1986.

Howell, Alan. "Building a Better Bridge." *International Journal of Frontier Missiology*, 32, no. 1 (2015).

Koné, Moussa. Memoir of an Imam. Lake Mary, FL: Creation House, 2013.

Love, Rick. *Muslims, Magic and the Kingdom of God*. Pasadena, CA: William Carey Library, 2003.

Musk, Bill. *The Unseen Face of Islam*. Oxford: Monarch, 2005.

Zwemer, Samuel. *The Influence of Animism on Islam: An Account of Popular Superstitions*. Trieste, 2017.

http://morethandreams.org/the-dreams/the-story-of-mohammed/.

BEYOND GREETINGS
&
TABLE MANNERS

An American teacher trained in the ways of the Navigators was working in a certain African university. Wanting to form a Navigator group from among the Christians there, he started a programme developed for use in the US. The first session was about self-image: who the participants saw themselves as individuals. The teacher found that it did not work as it was supposed to. He tried it several times. Eventually he told me, "These guys do not have a self-image."

Obviously, his conclusion lacked a certain professional rigour, but it flagged an unanticipated problem concerning the transfer of ideas and materials from one part of the world to another. The teacher was seeking to work with Christians. The problem he encountered was one of African culture, not of Christianity, and is relevant for African Muslims too.

What do we mean by "culture" here? Culture refers to a people's way of life, the system of values and perceptions they share, the rules they live by (that they actually live by, not just publicly affirm), the way they communicate, and so on. This is all learned behaviour rather than something they are born with. It is learned through being raised in a community. Geert Hofstede describes it as "software of the mind." Just as all children have an innate drive to learn the language of those around them, so we are all programmed to learn the codes of life and shared perceptions around us. We don't remember learning to speak as children. Speech just seems to come from inside us. In a similar way, we learn how life is: the unquestioned assumptions and unwritten rules of our community, the software for interacting with other people.

Just as languages can be radically different from each other, so can cultures. Our culture shapes what we understand about right and wrong. There is an unconscious layer, and then on top of that we build consciously and intentionally. Christian teaching and discipleship, by definition, is intentional and draws on sources that may conflict in some ways with our home culture. Until we have had to interact with different cultures, we often don't realise how much of our underlying culture comes through and shapes our understanding of Christianity. We read the Bible through lenses fashioned by our culture. We colour what we read with our own perceptions of the world. To use one very simple example, those of us who speak English habitually read "you" as singular and personal when promises and instructions are addressed to "you" as plural—that is, to whole groups and communities.

Consider this incident. It was a very hot Ramadan. The sun had set when Sameer appeared at the gate. I did not know him very well. He was a trainee teacher who was staying with a friend of mine. He came into the yard. He knew we had recently obtained a refrigerator. He had come with an empty bowl to ask if we could spare some ice.

"No problem," I said. "While I get it, please read this." I placed a Bible in his hands, which was opened to John 7:37–39.

On the last and greatest day of the festival, Jesus stood and said in a loud voice, "Let anyone who is thirsty come to me and drink. Whoever believes in me, as Scripture has said, rivers of living water will flow from within them." By this he meant the Spirit, whom those who believed in him were later to receive. Up to that time the Spirit had not been given, since Jesus had not yet been glorified.

I went inside, found some suitable cups of ice, released them into Sameer's bowl, and returned to him. He handed back the Bible, and without expression he said, "Now I know that Christianity is true and that Islam is false."

I was astonished. I had not expected such a response. "So you are going to become a Christian?" I asked.

Now it was his turn to be astonished. "No, of course not," he replied.

We looked at each other blankly for a moment. Then his face cleared. "Ah, I understand. You believe in personal choice. No, I am not going to become a Christian."

And he has not.

We all know that we need to learn the language and adapt to "the culture," but the culture is much more than forms of politeness and ways of eating. My misunderstanding that evening highlighted two elements. One was the significance of truth and the other was the individual's freedom to choose. I had assumed that when a person knew that his beliefs were false and that the truth was available, a change was inevitable. For Sameer, this was a surprising idea. I had assumed that he could change his allegiance. He was certain that it was not in his power to do so. Another way of casting this would be to say I believed that truth compelled him to change and he believed that his group identity compelled him to remain the same.

We are not going to do justice to the vast and wonderful subject of culture and all that is potentially involved in cross-cultural communication. Others have done that. Here we will point out things to look for and why they are important. Inevitably we will make some crude generalisations. These are to be taken as clues to be followed up rather than as a set of instructions.

I will contrast some typical Western characteristics with some typical African characteristics. I suspect this will still be relevant to non-Westerners if they have been subject to training that is of Western origin.

Here are some general headings:

AFRICA	WEST
Collective identity	Individualism
High context	Low context
High power distance	Low power distance
Patronage good	Patronage bad

We will unpack these terms in the following pages.

The Navigator at the beginning of this chapter was expecting to find a high sense of individual identity, because for him this would be absolutely normal. His assumption was that all people see themselves as individuals, as he himself did. Westerners typically introduce themselves first by name, then by what they do or by what organisation they work with. By contrast, many Africans traditionally introduce themselves first by their ethnicity and then by their village and other details, and their name comes last. (If that strikes us as sad and unbiblical, we need to look at how people in Bible times identified themselves to strangers; see Jonah 1:9; 1 Samuel 17:58; 30:13; 2 Samuel 1:8; Acts 21:39.) They understand themselves first and foremost as part of a group, whether that is tribe, clan, or household.

The extreme individualism that can be found in the West, in which members of the same family may develop totally different values and loyalties, is an oddity in human history; but for those raised in it, is normal. Despite generating diversity, it is still a culture, for parents nurture their children to make their own choices, to stand on their own two feet and find their own way. That is what they hold in common.

Cultures can be placed on a spectrum between strong individual identity and strong collective identity. Most African cultures are towards the collective end, and most Western cultures are towards the individualist end. There are some great presentations about these types of things on YouTube (see the list of additional resources at the end of this chapter).

INDIVIDUALISM	COLLECTIVISM
Society is a collection of individuals	An individual exists as part of the community.
Individual achievement is important. What *can* I do in the group?	Achievement of group is important. What *should* I do in our group?
Trust must be built.	Trust is a given. Don't lose it. Loyalty is a priority.
Work on harmony.	Maintain harmony.
Rules/regulations are the basis for the society or group.	Relationship is the basis of the society or group.

If people perceive themselves—first and foremost—as part of a group, this has far-reaching implications for how they live and how they experience life. Decisions about education, work, housing, and marriage are not made by the individual but by the group. In some cases, the individual may have no say at all. Even if power resides with the older generation, it is normally not an individual elder who decides. They consult with others at their level. However the younger people feel about it, they will in due course operate the same system when they are older, for it is normal and natural to them. Property is not individually owned; successes and failures are shared.

There is great emotional security in such a system when it is managed well. It can be abused, of course, as can any pattern of human interaction, including individualism. It is a profound mystery to many around the world how, in 2011, an insignificant and eccentric pastor, Terry Jones, could publicly burn Qur'ans in defiance of the president of his country—an extreme example of what can happen when rules protecting individual freedom are more important than obligations due to your ruler and country.

Islam is well adapted to collectivist culture. It brings a common code for all to submit to. It values corporate over private worship and the community over the individual. To make a very crude generalisation, the Arab culture in which Islam arose had a fairly strong collectivist dimension, but Africa even more so. For the vast majority in Africa, a person is a Muslim because his or her people are Muslim. This is not an individual choice. They might be good Muslims, they might be bad Muslims, but the Muslim identity itself is beyond negotiation.

All of this has important implications for cross-cultural communication of the gospel, especially if we have learned to present the gospel as the choice an individual must make. The description of Christ as "our personal Saviour" is a thoroughly Western idea and historically recent. Not only are individuals not authorised to choose their religious affiliation in most African Muslim cultures, but the very idea of individual personal salvation sounds wrong. It violates the conscience. To be sure, their history teaches them of Abraham, Moses, and Muhammad, who obeyed God and refused to follow the ways of their fathers, but it was always with the God-given purpose of calling the whole people to repentance and salvation. That is an Islamic theme that resonates in Africa. A message that appears to offer secret individual salvation sounds like seduction, not like truth.

No one should conclude that this collective approach to life is an impediment to the gospel. It is only a problem for Christians steeped in individualism. The book of Acts depicts a culture that was significantly more collectivist than Western evangelicals recognise. We find, at times, whole households coming to faith without every individual being personally approached. Acts 16:31–34 is a case in point.

Here are some of the implications.

1. The message should always explicitly address the group—indeed, the world—not just the individual we are talking to.

2. We need to learn to see the individual as part of the group. We need to be aware of what group the person belongs to. We need to cultivate the good opinion of those with significant influence.

3. In some cases, particularly small, well-defined communities, it is important to focus on the decision-making groups to the point of not being distracted by an eccentric individual who seems to respond. Our message loses credibility if we invest heavily in a dissident or youthful rebel setting himself against the people as a whole.

4. We should not expect a public change of identity as a seeker's first step of faith. Some speak of *discipleship before conversion*. This means that a person starts to follow Christ and to trust him while still a Muslim. The change of identity comes when the person has learned that Christ can be trusted and that a definitive choice is necessary.

5. If male trainee teachers and university students don't feel empowered to make major decisions, how much more so for young women, who are dependent on their fathers or husbands?

6. Ideally, the decision to change identity should be made together by a group—and, ideally, with the tacit blessing of some decision makers in the wider community. The gospel is divisive, but it does not necessarily lead to individualism.

7. Even when people do respond as individuals, they will assume they are joining a group, not just setting off on a solitary pilgrimage. This has implications for you, your family, and your associates. Westerners use the language of "brother" and "sister" lightly, without realising the power of those words in an African context, or indeed in the biblical context. To call someone "brother" or "sister" is to acknowledge a set of obligations and responsibilities that the African believer grasps fully. Muhammad, mentioned in chapter 1, assumed he should realign his life around his new family of believers and was met with confusion.

8. Persecution of new converts is not necessarily a manifestation of evil. From the point of view of the host community, it is good and morally right to apply pressure on an individual or group that deviates from their normal way of life. The fact that their social system does not acknowledge Christ as Lord and Saviour is, in a sense, a manifestation of residual evil, but many of the people who persecute will be motivated by love for the one who strays and by love for their family. A degree of persecution may be necessary to authenticate the reality of what God is doing both for the new believers and for the wider community. If the response of the persecuted is truly in accord with the teaching of Christ (in Matthew 5:10–11 and Matthew 5:38–48, for example), the persecution may well pass, some degree of reconciliation may follow, and others may be won over. As a general rule, in Africa family relationships are stronger than doctrine and religious affiliation.

9. New believers should be taught how to be a Christ-centred community, rather than how to cultivate their "personal walk." Since the conversion of the heart is central to Christian life and experience, there will always be an individual aspect. But, as in the New Testament, what is real in the heart is most clearly shown in how a disciple treats others rather than in devotion to codes, rules, texts, and doctrine.

A collectivist culture does not necessarily produce uniformity. There may be diversity of taste and practices. The strength of religious observance will vary across the group. Allowance is made for youth and circumstance. Nor is change always resisted. Every group wants something better, but it is measured in terms of benefit to the whole group, not just to the individual. What is primary is loyalty to the group itself.

TASKS, REFLECTIONS, AND MATTERS TO DISCUSS

Identify signs that suggest a collectivist outlook in approaches to work and education.

Find out how the choice of marriage partners is addressed. Who is responsible for raising children at different ages? (Do grandmothers or uncles have a particular role?)

Consider what God expects of people who believe but have no power to choose.

53

Does your message to those who do not yet believe violate the conscience of those with a sense of loyalty to their community?

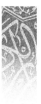 Consider what approaches might allow for the development of disciples within a given community?

Additional Resources

Hibbert, Evelyn, and Richard Hibbert. *Walking Together on the Jesus Road.* Pasadena, CA: William Carey Publishing, 2018.

Hofstede, Geert. *Cultures and Organizations: Software of the Mind.* New York: McGraw-Hill, 2010.

https://www.youtube.com/watch?v=CW7aWKXB5J4.

https://www.youtube.com/watch?v=GdPyrKVFMpA.

https://www.youtube.com/watch?v=RT-bZ33yB3c.

CONTEXT,
HIGH & LOW

I invited a local lay pastor, Ahmad, a former Muslim, to come and speak to a missionary fellowship. I gave him the time and the place. He agreed to come, but asked no questions. I say "but" because if our roles had been reversed, I would have asked a lot of questions. Do you want me to cover anything in particular? How long do you want me to take? How many people will be present? How formal will it be? Can I bring visual aids? Should I allow time for Q&A? For prayer? Will you introduce me?

Not knowing these things makes a person raised in a low-context culture nervous. Ahmad had no need to ask. He was accustomed to reading the context as he found it. For him the context was all about people, oneself, and one's relationships. Arrangements were going to be secondary to personal interaction. At best, they were guidelines. He was satisfied with his own understanding of why he had been invited. That was sufficient. He was raised high context; I was raised low.

Western cultures are typically low context and African cultures are typically high context. This refers to how people learn and how they interpret situations. In low-context cultures, information is passed explicitly in words. Decisions are recorded in writing; instructions are printed and have authority over what is merely remembered. Where explicit instructions are missing, the low-context person is insecure. In high-context cultures, children learn through observation and imitation much more than by being explicitly told.

I knew a Bible translator who was asked why she was always angry. Since she was not aware of having been angry at all, she was puzzled. She learned that in that particular culture people only asked direct questions out of anger. Although this is an extreme example, it is not out of character for high-context cultures.

Before we assume that we will learn about a people through interrogating some of its members, we need to have some idea about what emotional significance questions carry. He who asks inappropriate questions gets inappropriate answers and goes on his way calling it knowledge.

The table I am presenting here in regard to high and low context is adapted from Edward Hall.[3]

HIGH CONTEXT	LOW CONTEXT
Assumptions concerning communication	
Necessary information is to be found in the physical context or internalized in the person.	Most information is contained in explicit codes–either in verbal or written form.
The listener is already "contexted" and doesn't need to have much background information.	The listener knows very little and must be told practically everything.

3 Edward Hall, *Beyond Culture* (New York: Anchor, 1976).

Communication in practice	
The listener is responsible to understand the message, considering the whole context. The speaker tends to give simple, ambiguous messages.	**The speaker is responsible** for saying things in a clear, articulate way and tends to emphasize highly structured messages / give details / use correct wording.
Tends to use "feeling" in expression and to persuade.	Tends to use "logic" to present ideas and to persuade.
Is most at ease with indirect oral, rather than written, interaction.	Is most at ease with explicit, direct verbal and written communication.
Has extensive personal information networks.	Relies on explicit information sources, such as books, documents, policy manuals, etc.

High-context people use the skill of learning by observation rather than asking explicit questions and receiving explicit answers. When asked a question, they may respond with a story rather than a simple answer, because interpreting situations is how the listener gains understanding. Their world is not made up of definitions and neat rules, but of a complex web of relationships and realities. As adults, their experience of life has trained them to detect the signs regarding what is expected of them. Pause for a moment and consider this: Did Jesus lay out principles and then explain how they should be applied? Today, we are accustomed to reading what Jesus said and extracting or identifying principles. Jesus himself did not articulate principles. Look afresh at how he taught.

When African Muslims enter the home of a stranger, they read the house. Where are the places of honour? Where are the spaces set apart for men and where are those for women? They will know how to behave accordingly. When they enter the home of a Westerner, the signals are confused. The host does not expect them to find signals at all and gives them explicit instructions. "Please come this way." "Sit here." And then the host needs to ask explicit questions. "Would you like … ?" Muslim hosts, on the other hand, present what they expect the guest to accept and then read how they act in response.

When I arrive as a traveller in the home of a Westerner, I am usually supplied with an abundance of information. "The bathroom is here." "Help yourself to tea there." "Put your stuff there." "You will be sleeping in that room." "We will eat at seven, if that is OK."

If you were an African traveller arriving in an African home, you would most likely be told none of these things. You will be introduced to all the family. You will be seated and served. If others in the home don't speak your language, they might sit with you and talk among themselves rather than leave you on your own. Welcome is shown with body language, not with mere words.

But one might ask, if Pastor Ahmad is invited to address a group and totally misreads the situation, what happens then? The answer is that everyone covers for him. They are all working by the same rules. The relationships are more important than the arrangements. They do what they need to do so that no one is embarrassed. I have seen it happen.

African Islam is fully adapted to high-context culture. The first step into Islam for many traditional Africans is joining in the actions of the prayers, copying the ablutions, and then learning the words that must be said. Muslim life is laid out in patterns that are easy to see, such as distinctive clothing, a punctuated day, housing arrangements, and the use of special vocabulary. People learn to be Muslims by doing Islam. Clerics have disciples who learn by doing and obeying, not by asking questions and writing essays. The message is expressed in ritual actions. Their meaning does not need to be made explicit. A person's faith is made known by his or her actions and way of speaking, not by what he or she says. The Qur'an is memorised without understanding; how to behave as a Muslim is learned by example and conformity. In Africa, Islam succeeds without recourse to many of the things Westerners regard as essential to success.

This has important implications for the gospel and for discipleship. In my experience, some workers are highly informed about Islam and others are highly informed about cultural anthropology, but rarely are the two combined. They are taught as different subjects, but our business concerns people in whom these two come together.

One of the side effects of low-context workers entering a high-context environment is that the people in the host culture are conditioned to routinely look beyond the explicit words and actions to read the implied message. The low-context foreigners make everything they want to communicate explicit and evaluate their communication accordingly. Meanwhile, their hosts are busy decoding what the foreigners must really mean. Where no implicit message is given, one will be found anyway. Referring to a believer in a non-African high-context culture, Tim Green quotes a man who said, "All the time we were studying the Bible together, I was studying my teacher."

The low-context foreigner is accustomed to looking for explicit verbal responses and is likely to misinterpret or even completely overlook an implicit response. The local person probably has no idea that the foreigner is unable to read his or her indirect communication.

Many traditional approaches to sharing the gospel start with proving that the Bible has authority and then asserting what it says. In a high-context culture, this fails to persuade. If people are persuaded, it may not be because this method was used. The approach found in the Bible itself is different.

This does not mean that communication is impossible across such a cultural divide. Once we are alerted to it, we can learn. What is more, we have the example of Jesus to follow. We too need to learn how to tell parables. Translating the parables of Jesus is all right as far as it goes, but following the example of Jesus is better. He wrapped his message in parables. In other words, he made up stories to communicate what he wanted to say. So can we.

Jesus did not only give us an example of how to teach, he also instituted a ritual. The Lord's Supper, the Eucharist, the Mass, has been at the heart of Christian life and witness for centuries. The simple ceremony has been loaded down with rules and embellishments fought over by theologians and men of power, but it is packed with meaning. Ironically, the Christian communities most engaged in cross-cultural mission—namely, evangelicals—are those who (crude generalisation again) have the least appreciation for this powerful ritual. In fact, Western evangelicals are generally suspicious of rituals of all kinds. This is part of being extremely low context, although we may have well thought-out verbal reasoning to account for our position.

The Lord's Supper is so simple that a child can understand it and so deep that theologians can explore it for a lifetime. It is a practical reminder of the essential facts upon which the gospel is based. It speaks of the death, resurrection, and return of Christ. It provides a context for thinking about his purpose and significance. It addresses the individual heart, but it also forms the corporate nature of the community of Christ. It is a call to repentance and realignment. It is a proclamation of truth. It speaks to those suffering now. It reminds us of our dependence on Christ and his readiness to give himself.

The Lord's Supper embodies so much gospel truth. From time to time those truths can be taught explicitly and then repeated implicitly through regular practice. For cultures in which truth is normally encoded and expressed in rituals, the Lord's Supper is a wonderful tool. To be sure, it can be misused and misunderstood, but we should learn to appreciate it and use it.

TASKS, REFLECTIONS, AND MATTERS TO DISCUSS

 Find out how people say no to each other.

 Is it your experience that people say what they mean?

Do you find people telling you stories in answer to simple questions?

Find out from local people what visible actions show a person to be a good Muslim. What visible actions might show a person to be a follower of Christ?

 Discuss with your team the meaning of the Lord's Supper as it would come across to people in the local culture.

Additional Resources

Hibbert, Evelyn, & Richard Hibbert. *Walking Together on the Jesus Road.* Pasadena, CA: William Carey Publishing, 2018.

Zahniser, A. H. Mathias. *Symbol and Ceremony: Making Disciples across Cultures.* Monrovia, CA: MARC Publications, 1997.

http://www.culture-at-work.com/highlow.html.

https://www.youtube.com/watch?v=qKViQSnW-UA.

https://www.youtube.com/watch?v=VUSDEQspsm0.

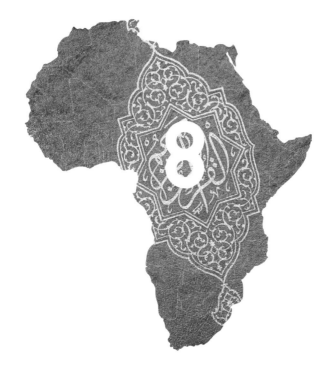

GUILT, SHAME, FEAR, & THE GOSPEL

The dynamics of honour and shame within a culture are increasingly being taken seriously in mission circles. If I might oversimplify—first it was largely ignored, then it was seen as a problem to solve. That led to the recognition that some cultures are very different to those in which our theology was developed. Eventually this has led to the realisation that the Scriptures too are full of honour-shame issues and that we in the West also have some learning to do. I do not have space here to fully explore this very important subject, but I will try to touch on the main points and apply them to Africa.

I take the view that honour-shame, law-guilt, and power-fear are all universal to human experience. They are all part of the human "operating system" upon which the programming of each culture runs. They are not harnessed to the same degree in all cultures. To illustrate with a different image, a dog depends most on its sense of smell to track its prey. It can hear and it can see, but scent is primary. For a cat, its eyes are primary. It can also hear and detect scent, but its eyes play a bigger role. The senses are not mutually exclusive. They complement each other, but they do so differently in different animals.

Honour-shame, law-guilt, and power-fear are all key dynamics within human cultures. Power-fear has not been taken as seriously as the others because of its association with "primitive" cultures. The assumption seems to be that progress eliminates it. I do not believe that this is either true or helpful.

Each dynamic influences behaviour and shapes, among other things, how right and wrong are handled. But they are not mutually exclusive. If you are raised in honour-shame, that does not mean you do not believe in law or guilt, but it does mean you relate to them differently. A sound desk has multiple sliding controls used to set different inputs and outputs. Every culture has a slider setting for each of these dynamics. On a scale of 1 to 10, honour-shame for one culture may be set at 8, law-guilt set at 2, and power-fear set at 3—so that is HS8 LG2 PF3. Another culture may be set at HS3 LG9 PF1.

The settings show the strength of each dynamic, and all societies have a setting for each. The combinations do not add up to 10, because the dynamics are not mutually exclusive. They are no more mutually exclusive than sight, hearing, and smell. Together they build sensory perception, on the basis of which a person acts.

The comparison with the senses is a useful one, because we use our basic cultural programming instinctively. People feel their way in an honour-shame culture. It also means that shame is not the equivalent of guilt. Shame may fulfil a role that someone from another culture expects to be filled by guilt, but it is not the same thing. Some have taken guilt-based gospel presentations and simply substituted the word *shame* for *guilt*. The result makes no sense. Each dynamic works differently.

Although guilt, shame, and fear are all feelings that a person may experience, we are talking here primarily about how cultures organise themselves. Guilt can be assigned to a person who does not feel it, and shame can be attached to someone who actually feels quite content, though shame often does have a big impact on emotions.

Generally speaking, in Africa the power-fear and honour-shame dynamics are much more powerful than the law-guilt dynamic. I will start here with law-guilt, not because it is better or higher but in order to show the contrasts.

In societies where the law-guilt dynamic predominates, there are explicit codes. Even when specific things are not codified, there is an assumption that they could be and should be. There is an underlying agreement that rules matter, that they should exist and be followed. People learn to feel and think in terms of guilt. Though not the only way, guilt is the primary way in which right and wrong are processed. Guilt is a response to the notion of law. Both law and guilt have power. Law and guilt combine to exercise a degree of control over behaviour. For this reason, I think law-guilt rather than guilt-innocence is the more helpful description. Innocence does not exercise power.

In societies where the power-fear dynamic predominates, people are conscious of powers that must be respected. This is most clearly seen in premodern, animistic societies, such as traditional Africa. However, it would be a serious mistake to imagine that the arrival of modern technology suppresses this dynamic. Today engineers and doctors are still aware of their vulnerabilities and the uncertainties of life. The powers may include the presence of ancestors, nature spirits, and invisible beings. Impersonal forces may also be significant. Observable things such as animals, storms, and fires are also to be taken into account. In power-fear societies, certain people are invested with authority, and these too are powers. The powers are largely unaccountable and cannot be predicted with confidence. Uncertainty is accepted as a fact of life—not an evil to be endured, but simply normal. Every aspect of life, every area of activity and decision making, is touched by this awareness.

The culture operates multiple strategies for dealing with the powers. The people follow codes of behaviour, engage in ritual, and practice avoidance; but the undesirable still happens and the cause is not readily apparent. There are so many possible causes. I previously mentioned the former marabout who had practiced African Islamic divination and traded in charms. His explanation that what the customer had obtained was good, but that someone else had bought something more powerful from another practitioner, was invariably accepted as a credible explanation.

How can I claim that this dynamic is universal? If we look at our own Western culture a little more closely, we see that superstitions persist, astrology will not go away, sportsmen follow lucky rituals, parents fear jinxing their kids by saying the wrong thing, belief in fate is profound, and the scientific narrative that says we are all controlled by unaccountable genes finds a ready audience. The settings on the slider may be low, but the dynamic is nevertheless present in Western societies too.

Power and the fear of power are motivators for behaviour. The opposite of fear is peace, or perhaps security, which are certainly desired states, but in themselves inert. It is the interaction of fear and power that generates behaviour. One of the cultural forms that is generated is law—that is, basic rules for life—but the rules and codes of societies dominated by the power-fear dynamic are usually ambiguous. In law-guilt societies, wrestling with wording to eliminate ambiguity and uncertainty is considered a good use of time. Even laws submit to law—a law is only valid if it keeps the rules. This is not the case in power-fear cultures. The rules and codes are important strategies for dealing with reality, but the reality is stronger and only submits to a limited degree. No law is absolute. No one expects to be in control.

One of the features of this kind of approach is that what we call moral issues are put in together with ecological and ethnic issues. All the rules, taboos, and required actions form part of a whole. Failing to offer food to a long-departed ancestor or not respecting a crocodile are on the same level as failures of honesty or personal integrity. It is not that all responsibilities are necessarily rated equally—far from it—but rather that they all rest on the same nonmoral basis. Or to put it another way, the thing that is really immoral is to do (or fail to do) something which leads to the community being put at risk. The human conscience processes life in those terms. People's guilt is more about the consequences than the actions per se, and actions for which there are no consequences generate no feelings of guilt.

Before we can outline honour-shame culture, we need to recognise that there are at least two quite different types of culture in which honour-shame is dominant. No one could describe Egyptian and Japanese cultures as being similar, but in both cultures honour-shame is very prominent. Japan's culture is such that the crime rate is astonishingly low. Murder is rare, but suicide is relatively high. Egypt has plenty of crime, but few suicides. Both are quite definitely honour-shame cultures, but they have different criteria for honour and different ways of dealing with shame.

My point is that honour-shame is not just one thing. In fact, although the two things are related, they are not simply two sides of one coin. If it were possible to put a numerical value on someone's shame, that would not mean you would be able to take that figure and calculate their honour, nor vice versa. It is never as simple as that. This is a very rich area to explore in other cultures, in our own, and in Scripture.

Honour is a form of wealth. It is desirable. It offers security. It may be inherited, or it may be earned. It concerns the reputation of both the group and the individual. Cultures in which honour-shame is the dominant dynamic are usually more collectivist than individualist. They tend to be high context rather than low. But these spectrums are not the same thing as honour-shame. In honour-shame societies, a person may well forfeit money to retain honour, or even sacrifice life to gain honour.

Shame is hugely important in many cultures. In some ways, it is like a financial deficit. When you are deep in debt, it may be very hard to get out of it. The fact of financial debt handicaps those so afflicted, regardless of the cause. Whether it is your own fault or an inherited debt, the result is the same. Shame, disgrace, and dishonour are hard to shift. Fear of shame is a powerful motivator toward approved behaviour. Fear of it can also drive deceit and denial.

Shame, like honour, can be inherited, gained, and lost. Unlike power-fear and law-guilt, this pair of opposites can drive each other; it is not a case of one being the stimulant and the other being the response, but the relative power of each varies from one culture to another. Hunger for honour and fear of shame are both powerful motivators. The equivalent of power or law in this case is public opinion. But public opinion is fluid and unstable. It is not the real generator. It awards honour and shame as a response to stimulus. It is merely reactive.

Honour and shame are attached to people. They are not abstractions, like legal codes or taboos. They are ascribed to persons, both individuals and groups. Aspects of honour-shame permeate every aspect of life. They constitute a dimension in every relationship. The whole culture is very relational. Who you buy your groceries from has more to do with relationship than price. Even the price you are willing to pay may be an expression of status, in stark defiance of Western economic theory. Everyone is sensitive to the worth of others, and failing to acknowledge someone's worth may be a serious issue, even for persons in humble circumstances.

Power-fear is certainly a significant dynamic for many African Muslims. God is one of the powers, theoretically the supreme power, but other unaccountable powers are allowed to operate too. Rituals and taboos are also observed to try to assure a good harvest, a profitable day at the market, or success in exams. Blood sacrifice is made to bring success in farming and other work. People invest in charms. African Islam makes room for multiple strategies for dealing with unaccountable powers. There is a place for anything that seems to yield results. Western medicine, traditional healing, and divination go on side by side. The state is respected, but its laws are negotiated according to circumstances. Those who wield state power, whether governors, mayors, or local policemen, exercise it according to a variety of factors, not as servants of a system with tight rules.

Honour-shame is also a significant dynamic. In many African cultures, fear of shame seems much more important than pursuing honour. It is as though everyone starts out with a default level of personal honour, which must be defended. Any slight or offence causes hurt and needs remedy. Showing respect is of paramount importance and is needed for normal interaction. Overt competition for honour seems to be minimal. At the same time, groups within the culture have different levels of honour compared to each other. Hierarchy is normal, but any competition between groups is usually hidden. The sort of culture that one finds in the Middle East, in which open competition for honour between individuals and between groups is normal and aggressive, is found in Africa too, but is, I think, much less common. The generally held priority of harmony is much stronger. The power-fear dynamic goes well with that priority for harmony.

The display of honourable status through clothing and etiquette is pretty common. People within a community know what is expected of people of different social rank, and violation of that expectation is an honour-shame issue. Strangers are also expected to sense these things, and one of the most universal causes of offence by outsiders in Africa is the failure to show respect where respect is due.

In some honour-shame cultures, all perceived slights to one's honour are met with open anger and aggression. In others, anger is suppressed and expressed indirectly in gossip or through coldness and aloofness. In each case, the response is deemed appropriate to the offence. Generally, the high value set on self-control in Africa means that open anger as a strategy is much less common (but not unknown!).

In some cultures, the power of shame is demonstrated by people exiling or destroying themselves if they are shamed or bring shame on their people. In others, there is an unflinching denial of wrongdoing even in the face of clear evidence. Both are ways of dealing with shame. In my experience, denial seems to be the more common approach in African cultures, but workers should discover how things work in the culture in which they find themselves. The resolution of conflicts between two injured parties, whether individuals or groups, requires much more than a review of the facts of the case. And I should add that since no one is truly an isolated individual, there is always a group element to every personal conflict. He who insults my brother insults my people.

What Are the Implications for the Gospel?

People do have an awareness of need, of separation from God, but it is not usually expressed in terms of guilt. Some workers have concluded that what the people need is to be instructed so that they rightly understand what their need really consists of. I would say that the Scriptures give us reasons to respect different understandings of human need.

As I have become aware of the richness of the account of the Fall in Genesis 3, I have also become acutely aware of how many ways Westerners twist it and rewrite it to make it say what they want it to say while sincerely believing they are faithfully relaying God's truth. The Fall account is remarkable. It speaks powerfully to every culture.

What do you find if you are a power-fear person? Adam and Eve are in an ideal environment, living in peace and plenty without fear. There is but one taboo. Our imaginary reader does not need an explanation as to why the tree should be forbidden. He or she needs no philosophical explanation about freedom and the nature of love. The existence of a taboo seems entirely normal.

The all-powerful God was their protector and friend. Then they did the one thing that they ought not to do, and everything changed. This makes sense too. Suddenly they became afraid. They knew fear for the first time. The Creator approached them with questions. In many power-fear cultures, questions are only asked if something is wrong. They hid. They had no effective way to disguise what they had done. They were vulnerable and naked. The result was that they forfeited the safe environment of Eden and found themselves in a harder world, exposed to the elements and other powers. They were cut off from the tree of life. They were now exposed to death.

There is much more that could be said, especially about their inability to resist evil and the presence of temptation. The passage speaks the language of power-fear.

Readers raised in honour-shame also find a story that speaks their language. Adam and Eve enjoyed a high status in the created world and good standing with the patron of all. They were recipients of great favour, blessed in every way. (There may have been no public to affirm their status as people of honour within the account, but the story is written for a public which looks back at them and recognises it nonetheless). Honour-shame cultures are fundamentally relational, and in Genesis the first relationships were sweet and undefiled. To go against the express wishes of your benefactor is always a serious matter. To be unfaithful to your creator by listening to an enemy is shameful, and this is what they did.

As a consequence, they experienced shame and fear. Inevitably they were caught. Their failing was exposed. When confronted, they tried to save face by passing the blame. How so like us! What were the consequences? Loss of privileges, loss of standing, loss of access, permanent demotion, doomed to mortality. And as honour-shame people would expect, the new status was inherited by their children.

In some ways, our Western law-guilt culture has the hardest time reading the passage. We immediately ask: Why was the tree there? Or why was the snake there? Neither question is answered by Scripture, but many Western presentations, even to non-Westerners, feel compelled to answer these questions as part of the basic presentation. We feel insecure with the story as it is told.

So what do we find, reading as law-guilt people? There was a perfectly reasonable law. Adam and Eve broke that law. When laws are broken, there must be consequences. Now the sentence was death. Many preachers say that the sentence was partially carried out and that Adam and Eve "died spiritually," a phrase that makes absolutely no sense in Old Testament terms. The apparent similarity with Ephesians 2 is misleading.

Anyway, Adam and Eve felt guilt and sought to evade the judge. As guilty people—sinners—they were excluded from paradise. They could not undo what had been done. Their offence was inexcusable. Why it should be that Adam and Eve's offspring also suffer the punishment earned by their parents before their birth is hard to explain in law-guilt terms. Some make up for this by suggesting that Adam and Eve's nature was changed and passed on.

I have intentionally not yet picked up on God's provision of clothing made from animal skins. Of course, many gospel communicators take the opportunity to draw out the implication that an animal had to die, prefiguring sacrifice. That may have some merit, but it has to be said that no Scripture writer ever makes such a link. If we are to read sacrifice into it, then what did the sacrifice achieve? It did not expiate the sin, though it may have been part-payment, saving them from immediate death, for they still died.

Many Westerners say that God can have no relationship with sinners, and that at the Fall Adam and Eve were utterly separated from God. However, in the story, after having passed judgement on them, God made them clothes, better clothes than they could make for themselves. He demonstrated kindness towards them. In Genesis 4, God gives advice to Cain, a man whose sacrifice he had already rejected. The narrative that has sinners utterly separated from a holy God is not supported by these texts—quite the reverse.

From a power/fear point of view, these things do not present a problem. Because of their lack of respect for the power, Adam and Eve have to live in a more dangerous world. But despite their disobedience, God still shows kindness by covering their nakedness and protecting them from the elements. The level of favour is lower, but there is hope. Since God is still their benefactor, they still have obligations to him. What is absolutely fascinating is that all the themes of the Fall, from whichever angle you view them, recur in the death and resurrection of Christ.

On the cross, Jesus took the place of the weak—helpless before the power. He took the place of the disgraced. He took the place of the law-breaker. Yet he was in himself strong, honourable, and innocent. He was there of his own free will in obedience to the Father. Fear and shame systems often resolve issues through ritual sacrifice, and Christ was that sacrifice. Law systems require a sentence to be carried out, and we see that too. In his resurrection, Jesus showed that he had defeated every power. He was shown to be the one honoured by God over against all the other authorities that conspired against him. Our preoccupation with his divinity obscures the truth that he is a fellow human, now seated on high; and our Western individualism makes it hard for us to appreciate that those associated with him thereby share in his honour and glory, whatever the world may say. In his ascension, Christ was accorded the highest honour that there can ever be and appointed judge of the living and the dead. In the resurrection, he was also vindicated, declared innocent of all charges by the higher judge. The events of the atonement speak powerfully in all three dynamics.

What Are the Implications for Discipleship?

Rightly understood, discipleship is about learning to live in the way of Christ before God, along with other believers in the world. The way of Christ seriously challenges all patterns derived from the three dynamics.

Law-guilt people have to learn to set their rights aside and become servants. They have to learn to forgive freely and to repent of judging others.

Honour-shame people have to learn that the only honour that counts is the honour that God bestows and that the way of true honour may incur the scorn of the unbelievers. It is the servant who is honoured, not the person who exalts himself.

The power-fear person has to learn to live in the knowledge that God is Father, that God is good, and that all powers are subject to Christ. Security lies in trusting God alone and obeying him. Harmony with the world is not guaranteed, nor is it to be sought as the highest priority.

This brief introduction to this vital aspect of life does not tell anyone what they can expect in any particular context. It only suggests some key things to be looking for and some clues about what strategies might be needed.

TASKS, REFLECTIONS, AND MATTERS TO DISCUSS

 Observe how people dress, especially those who are wealthy. What do you notice?

 Observe how police officers behave. Do they apply the law equally to all? Ask people you know what they think. Ask if they have ever been treated leniently by a police officer, and if so, why that might be.

Find out what is involved in resolving personal conflicts. Is their way or resolving conflict different to the ways you are used to?

How freely do people admit that they are wrong? How freely do they speak of the wrong done by someone associated with them?

What indication is there in the culture that people are aware of their need of God?

Additional Resources

Georges, Jayson. *Ministering in Honor-Shame Cultures: Biblical Foundations and Practical Essentials.* Downers Grove, IL: IVP Academic, 2016.

Mischke, Werner. *The Global Gospel.* Scottsdale, AZ: Mission ONE, 2014.

Muller, Roland. *The Messenger, the Message, the Community,* especially part 2. CanBooks, 2013.

http://honorshame.com.

https://sahelchurchplanter.wordpress.com/2017/08/31/honour-shame-fear-and-the-gospel-of-god/.

http://wernermischke.org/resources/.

WHAT ARE FRIENDS *FOR?*

Sadiq was angry, even bitter. He could say nothing good about James, a missionary and his former employer. Working as a night guard had suited Sadiq well. He had plenty of time to read the Scriptures and learn from James. Now he had been cast off over some matters of punctuality and other trivial matters. As for James, he had, with a heavy heart, "let Sadiq go." He had thought employing him would be a great opportunity both to disciple him and help him support his family. And for a while it was. But the relationship had broken down. Sadiq had become hard in his attitude. He was no longer carrying out his agreed duties in the manner expected.

Both parties felt themselves wronged. Sadiq's feeling was much stronger and more enduring. What had happened? Each had failed the expectations of the other. James had no idea that for Sadiq the employment contract was a formality, that the real rules they were operating by were the unwritten rules of patronage. From Sadiq's point of view, James had behaved disgracefully.

SIL worker Harriet Hill, writing some years ago in *Ethos,* said the following:

> Stepping off the plane in Africa, we should be greeted by large posters saying "welcome to the land of patron-client systems." It would help us all to get along better. It seems to be a common feature across the continent and in some countries, e.g., Kenya, a type of friendship other than patron-client is hardly known.

Such a poster would not help much because many of us, especially those of us coming from the West, would not grasp its significance. In the West, patronage is not a term with a positive image. It is something we treat with suspicion. However, in much of the world today, as in the civilisations of the past, patronage is a normal part of everyday life. It is immensely important in Africa. And let us not overlook the fact that Hill was not just talking about political systems or trading arrangements. She was talking about friendships. When we arrive in a foreign culture, we know we have to learn a new language and new ways of being polite, but we tend to assume that we know what friendship is, how it works, and what it is for.

What is patronage? Patronage describes a reciprocal relationship between two persons of unequal status that involves the exchange of different kinds of goods and services. While that description is not inaccurate, it does not paint a full enough picture. Patronage occurs in an environment in which everyone is aware of and accepts inequality as normal. Such inequality is not a problem to be solved; it is a fundamental part of how the world works. Seeking and giving patronage are strategies for navigating that inequality. Friendships are made with this in mind. Local people do not need classes in how to practice patronage; it is a part of their understanding of life. Patronage thinking resides in subconscious attitudes.

Patronage is about relationships, about the obligations that flow from being related to another person—whether that relationship arises from kinship, proximity, employment, or choice. Patronage is an expression of interdependence. Within immediate family and among neighbours, interdependence is the norm. In traditional Africa, no one seeks to be independent of others. Interdependence is seen as desirable, in addition to being necessary. Any person who seeks to be autonomous is morally suspect.

This is in sharp contrast to the prevailing attitude in the West. We want to do as much as we can on our own and to be self-reliant. We want our children to become independent from us, able to stand on their own two feet, to make their own living. Parents provide for their own old age and do not want to be a burden on their children. Such attitudes are reflected in popular proverbs such as "If you want something done right, do it yourself" and "God helps those who help themselves."

David Maranz, author of *African Friends and Money Matters,* writes:

> Africans I have talked to about this are not used to thinking in terms of what they can do by themselves with their own resources. They have always managed the whole of their life, including their finances, in relationship with family and friends. To them suggesting that they begin thinking in terms of living independently or autonomously, without receiving from and giving to others, is foreign and worse than unattractive … Long-term interdependent relationships are at the heart of being African. … Africans want and expect to depend upon others and they want others to depend upon them.

Such attitudes are reflected in proverbial sayings like these:

> The remedy for man is man.
>
> A person is a person through people.
>
> It is because of the tree that the liana was able to climb up.
>
> The right hand washes the left, and the left the right.
>
> One finger does not catch a louse.
>
> One head does not sit in council.
>
> As a snake lives with soil so a person lives with his/her countrymen.
>
> The axe does not sharpen itself.
>
> I have taken care of you up to the time you cut your teeth; you now take care of me because I am losing mine.

A sentiment often expressed in America goes, "If you want to make an enemy of family or friends, loan them money." People borrow items and return them as quickly as possible. By contrast, as my colleague Hans Rothenburger puts it, "In Africa, people want to borrow and lend in order to be functioning, contributing, and respected members of society. People want to be owed money by their friends. A person without outstanding credits is friendless and without recourse in the day of trouble."

Patronage was part of the way of life in Jesus' time too. As an approach to life, it is neither good or bad; it is possible to abuse it, and sinners do. It is also possible to behave righteously as a patron or as a client. The early church included people who were unequal in status and resources. By regarding each other as kin-through-faith they applied the rules of familial interdependency to their fellowship as believers. Jesus had laid the foundations to this approach in calling people to set the kingdom and loyalty to his person above obligations to biological family (e.g., Matt 12:46–50; 23:8–9; Luke 14:26).

The style of discipleship used by Jesus that we see in the Gospels is a variety of patronage. Disciples attached themselves to, and were accepted by, a master. The disciple was both learner and servant—ready to obey, acknowledging the master's superior knowledge and power. Jesus specifically taught how kingdom-style interdependence should work differently by showing that even the master sees himself as a servant, though he is still "teacher and Lord."

While living in Africa, we become part of the system there whether we recognise it or not. Simply as people with connections abroad, we are marked as people with power. We are also, to some extent, dependent on local people. There is much we do not know. We have to deal with officials who have the ability to make life very difficult for us. We are the customers of shopkeepers. Our relationship with them is an unequal one.

In the Western world, we try to depersonalise all these relationships and expect rules to govern our interactions. In Africa, it is the opposite. Every interchange is personal and has the potential to be a beneficial relationship between persons. Dishonest officials exploit their power— sometimes by being hostile and sometimes by being friendly! Honourable officials are helpful not just because it is their job, but because they want to make friends with other honourable people. That is patronage.

There is nothing ungodly about interdependence, though at times it produces stresses and strains. Those who have more can use their position for good to benefit those who need it, or they can abuse their power to benefit themselves and their associates with a disregard for the interests of others. The culture of patronage is not unbiblical, but sinful people find many opportunities in it to do wrong. Similarly, sinful individualistic people find plenty of opportunities to do wrong in their individualist, independence-loving culture.

If we are calling people to follow Christ in Africa, they are going to be doing so within this system of interdependence and patronage. We cannot rewrite the culture for them, nor should we, for there is nothing fundamentally wrong with it. Scripture addresses people living in just such a culture and does not train them to become Western individualists.

In my experience, Westerners try to make themselves as independent as possible from local people. They prefer to drive their own vehicles and are careful with their possessions. They may secure their own water supply, and they shop around for the best deal. They do not like to be asked for money. They regard their time as a commodity to be tightly managed. Local people sense it. Africans share their time, food, and possessions much more easily as a normal part of being interdependent people. They regularly buy from the same stores and market stalls so that the buyer and seller have a connection. To be asked for advice, help, or money is seen positively, as an opportunity to strengthen a bond.

My colleague Eliki, who was from the South Pacific, had a different feel for relationships than the rest of our team. One day he was shopping in the main market and realised he did not have enough money with him. He went to Ali, a prosperous shopkeeper whom he often bought from, and asked him to lend him some cash. Ali was pleased to be asked and handed it over readily. No one else on the team would have thought to do that. Giving and receiving favours is how relationships are forged. We need to learn to do it their way.

Discipleship is a two-way process. The way people respond to us is shaped by local patronage expectations concerning what is appropriate towards the patron. We are involved in a relationship with persons, not engaging in a mere transmission of information. We call believers brothers and sisters. Those words carry a much greater implication in Africa than they do in the West, and our understanding of them is much further away from the biblical meaning than theirs is.

81

Unscrupulous people may attach themselves to us insincerely, saying all the right things to win our trust. That is an ever-present hazard. The solution is not to isolate ourselves, but rather to seek to establish solid friendships with reliable people of good reputation and to listen to their advice. They see through our false friends more easily than we do.

Honest, sincere people will attach themselves to us if we are seen to be honourable. They want community, not just a doctrine. We need to learn to understand them so that we do not fail them. If we fail to treat them in the way that the wider community regards as right, we and our message are both discredited. Yes, this is a minefield. But it is not just about avoiding mistakes; it is about realising the potential. These are people who know in theory how to make community work—even if they have not followed their own codes in the past—and by embracing the love and faith of Christ theirs can become gloriously healthy communities.

It has become fashionable to speak of seeking a "person of peace." Africans who are seeking something, seek for the person who can give them access. The people whom God is preparing may also be seeking a person of peace themselves. Whether you are recognised as one depends on whether you meet their criteria.

TASKS, REFLECTIONS, AND MATTERS TO DISCUSS

Observe who people count as friends.
Do they mainly trust people they are related to?

To what extent are you dependent on local people?
How do you feel about that?

Find out if discipleship is practiced in the culture.
Do people learn skills through apprenticeship?
If so, what are the expectations in terms of relationships?

 What would make someone identifiable in their eyes as a "person of peace?"

Additional Resources

de Silva, David. *Honor, Patronage, Kinship and Purity: Unlocking New Testament Culture.* Downers Grove, IL: IVP Academic, 2000.

Howell, Alan B., and Robert Andrew Montgomery. "God as Patron and Proprietor: God the Father and the Gospel of Matthew in an African Folk Islamic Context." *International Journal of Frontier Missiology* 36, no. 3 (2019).

Maranz, David. *African Friends and Money Matters.* 2nd ed. Dallas: SIL International, 2015.

"WE PREACH CHRIST CRUCIFIED" (1 COR 1:23)

Muslims in Africa, like Muslims everywhere else in the world, reject the assertion that Christ died on a cross and was raised again. Workers preparing to engage with Muslims learn about this issue and the various ways of affirming the historical facts of the matter, along with its significance for us and for them. The death and resurrection of Christ are fundamental to our message. What many workers seem to be less conscious of is that our own understanding of the atonement has been shaped by our culture.

The Scriptures speak of the atonement in a variety of ways, and in our own context particular themes, interpretations, and explanations have been brought into sharp focus. We affirm and defend these interpretations and explanations with the same zeal as the historical facts because we do not recognise which is which. When we are taking the message into a radically different culture with its own understanding of God and the world, it is helpful not only to return to Scripture but also to recognise that our theology shapes what we think the Scriptures teach. We have lenses of which we are unconscious. This is not an attempt to accommodate Islam, but to set aside perspectives that have been helpful in the West but may be unhelpful in our new context.

Theology is the result of people asking serious questions that were not explicitly addressed in the Scriptures. For example, the apostles proclaimed Christ as the divine Son of God. In the following centuries, the church wrestled with how to understand the nature of Christ in relation to the one God. The apostles did not seem to feel the need to resolve the logical questions that arose from their teaching, but those issues became central to later generations. Various formulations were proposed, some of which were accepted and some of which were not. All of them were attempts to make sense of the New Testament witness to Christ.

Many years ago, I attempted to put together a gospel presentation using only statements explicitly made in the New Testament. I made some disturbing discoveries. Working solely from the New Testament, I could find no explicit, unambiguous statements to support certain things which I "knew" to be true. This included expressions I was accustomed to singing in church every week. Over time, the list has lengthened. Among these are that Jesus was punished in our place, the wrath of God was poured out on Christ, a holy God can have no relationship with sinners, the Father turned his back on the Son, and that a just God cannot simply forgive sinners without someone being punished.

These expressions are so widely used that to read what I have just written can be a shock. This is not to say that these familiar statements are false, only that they are not stated in Scripture in that form. They contain an element of explanation or elaboration that has been helpful in our tradition.

The culture of individualism in the West and the culturally driven need to be able to explain rationally how everything fits together underly some of the explanations that shape our understanding of what the text says.

These are some of the things that Muslims in Africa honestly find hardest to understand. Many of the scriptural statements are actually ambiguous. "Christ died for sinners." Does that mean because of sinners or for the benefit of sinners? "Christ died for sins." As a result of sins? Because of sins? The sins of all or the sins of some? As full judicial payment or as a symbolic but effective ritual?

In the evangelical world, these issues have been addressed vigorously in the past, arguing from the Scriptures first against Roman Catholic and then against liberal positions. The resulting explanations, taught as the true message of the apostles, are the explanations that resonate with Christians in our own culture. Our culture asks how individuals can be saved and be sure that they are saved. Until very recently, the awareness of alienation from God in the West was primarily understood in terms of guilt rather than shame or powerlessness. In fact, we train ourselves to read the Scriptures through the lenses of guilt, which is why we do not see the other aspects of the Fall discussed in chapter 8.

The Western culture asks questions about free will that many cultures simply do not ask, and answering those questions runs through our theology. I have seen audio-visual gospel presentations used across Africa in which it was felt essential to address the issue of free will right from the beginning. This was a reflection of the culture that presentation came from, not of the culture of those being addressed.

It came as a surprise to me, as I find it does to many of my colleagues, that there have been several theories of atonement over the centuries, each of which sought to faithfully represent scriptural teaching. Here I am going to give a quick overview of atonement theories in the hope that readers will look more deeply into them for themselves.

For most of the first millennium of Christianity, the dominant atonement theory was "Christus Victor"—the idea that Christ defeated sin and death by his death and resurrection and that he was able to save because he was Lord of all. In the third century, Origen flirted with the idea that the atonement was a payment to the devil, but that view did not take root. Throughout that extended period, the main theme was that Christ had brought salvation to Adam's race by defeating evil once and for all. The focus was very much on humankind, not on the individual. The individual benefitted, but was not the focus. Salvation was "located" in Christ, not in people.

In the eleventh century, questions were being explored about why the cross was necessary and what exactly made it effective. In answer to these questions, Anselm propounded the Satisfaction Theory. He argued that the cross was necessary for God. Humanity's sin was an offence to God's honour. Just as a feudal lord could not simply overlook gross offences, nor could God. Jesus had to suffer as a representative of Adam's race so that the rest might be pardoned. The cross met God's need.

Anselm was a grand old man, one of the great intellects of his age. His position was opposed by Peter Abelard, a brilliant young upstart. Abelard asked how humanity murdering God's Son could lessen the offence of sin. He argued that if God could not forgive without someone suffering, Jesus should not have been able to pronounce forgiveness on people he met. He argued that only a cruel person could require an innocent to be killed before being merciful to the guilty. He proposed the Exemplar or Moral Influence Theory, which focussed on the cross as a demonstration of the love of God which inspires a response. The cross was necessary for humankind.

In Reformation times, Anselm's theory was developed and adapted. According to the Penal Substitution Theory, it was not God's honour that needed satisfaction, but rather the Law or God's righteousness or holiness. Such an approach has become the orthodoxy in evangelical circles. It has a particular focus on how an individual soul is saved and understands human need in terms of guilt. This view resonated with the underlying culture. The Abelard-type approach resurfaced later in liberal theology, but also in some more evangelical authorities, such as Hugo Grotius in the sixteenth century and much more recently in Kenneth Bailey, the celebrated expositor of Middle Eastern culture.[4]

In nineteenth-century animist Africa, Western missionaries preached about guilt and penal substitution. But many times it was other elements of the gospel that caught the imagination of their hearers, especially the idea that the estranged creator God should take the initiative in effecting reconciliation. Blood sacrifice was a familiar part of traditional religious life, but was not understood as being primarily about sin. To this day, African churches tend to embody a Christus Victor approach. I make this admittedly sweeping generalisation in the hope that my readers will observe African churches for themselves and draw their own conclusions.

---

4 See Kenneth Bailey, *Paul through Mediterranean Eyes* (London: SPCK Publishing, 2011), chapter 5.

African Muslims combine their underlying African culture with Islamic thinking and practice. For Muslims, the creator God has intervened in human history and provided a religion by which they seek to live in right relationship with him and with each other. Their faith is an international one, not so easily undermined by the arrival of the modern world in the way that localised tribal cults were.

If African Muslims are to take the gospel seriously, it must make sense to them. Generally speaking, penal substitution does not. An approach that seems to be about solving God's problem simply does not resonate. A message that seems to offer personal salvation rather than community salvation feels wrong. A solution for personal guilt is a remedy for a problem that is simply not high on their agenda.

This does not mean that such themes are invalid, but it does mean that it is unhelpful to put these things front and centre in messages addressed to not-yet-believers. The gospel has other aspects and elements that may persuade them more readily if the message is to be taken seriously.

Missions have responded to this challenge by re-educating the unsaved through chronological storytelling, painting a vivid Bible-based picture in which sin, guilt, and sacrifice are prominent. Jesus comes to meet the need portrayed in this retelling of history. Although the approach is Scripture-based, the stories are actually embellished with explanations and interpretations to bring out the desired themes according to the presenter's particular theology. Proponents of this approach hardly notice they are doing it. They just want to bring out the truth.

The Scriptures speak the languages of honour-shame and of power-fear. They also speak to collective identity far more than we realise. It is false to assume that because Muslims do not accept the doctrine of original sin that they have no awareness of their need before God. Muslim seekers always have much to learn; it is unfortunate if we require them to learn things that not only go against their understanding of life but are themselves expressions of Western reasoning rather than eternal truth.

The Apostle Paul famously asserted, "We preach Christ crucified: a stumbling block to Jews and foolishness to Gentiles, but to those whom God has called, both Jews and Greeks, Christ the power of God and the wisdom of God" (1 Cor 1:23–24). We have become accustomed to understanding this as meaning that the crucifixion is central, the resurrection only serving to confirm it. So much evangelical preaching and teaching has focussed on *how* the cross works. That is not what this text meant to Paul or his readers. "We preach Christ" carries with it the intended implication that we are speaking of a living person, for a dead Messiah is by definition not a Messiah at all. That the Messiah should reign forever was basic to the job description.

"Crucified" is a past passive participle—that is to say, Christ was once crucified. The idea of a divinely sanctioned Lord and Saviour who had passed through a humiliating execution and now lives to rule and save was indeed foolishness to Greeks and a stumbling block to Jews. Nevertheless, it spoke powerfully into both cultures in different ways, as is evidenced by the growth of the early church.

Western culture is undergoing change. Theology is under pressure to change too. Liberalism is one alternative approach that has arisen and is increasingly seen to have failed. It would be a mistake to assume that every challenge to evangelical orthodoxy is liberal in origin. A solid commitment to the integrity of the Scriptures and sincere faith in the living Lord Jesus when faced with the questions that arise from a different cultural environment can and should give rise to a fresh understanding. The object should still be to hold to the faith once entrusted to the saints; but that requires a fresh look at the first century, not just the sixteenth.

TASKS, REFLECTIONS, AND MATTERS TO DISCUSS

Write down, as briefly as you can, the essentials of the gospel as you understand them. Then compare that with what was preached in Acts to non-believers. What items are absent from your list but present in Acts? What items are present on your list but absent from Acts? How can these differences be accounted for?

Since it is normal for unbelievers to reject the gospel unless they are enlightened by the Spirit, does it matter how we express its truths? Does Matthew 7:12 have any relevance to how we communicate?

Discuss how the people you are serving understand their need before God. In what ways does "your gospel" address their understanding of their need?

Additional Resources

Baker, Mark D., and Joel B. Green. *Recovering the Scandal of the Cross: Atonement in New Testament and Contemporary Contexts.* Downers Grove, IL: IVP Academic, 2011.

Beilby, James, and Paul R. Eddy, eds. *The Nature of the Atonement: Four Views.* Downers Grove, IL: IVP Academic, 2006.

Wright, N. T. *How God Became King: The Forgotten Story of the Gospels.* New York: HarperOne, 2016.

AN
APPROPRIATE
MESSAGE

The preaching of Peter in Acts 2, of Stephen in Acts 7, and of Paul in Acts 13 have something in common. They all spent most of the time telling their listeners things that they already knew. The new information, "the good news," followed a reminder of the already familiar. As a rule, African Muslims are not familiar with the biblical narrative, so reminding them of it makes no sense. Therefore, some workers prefer to supply it first— that is, they teach the whole Bible chronologically as preparation for the good news.

However, in Acts we read that the apostles also met people such as the Athenians who had no previous scriptural knowledge. In such cases, they used a different starting place for their message. The messages in Acts, whether addressed to the biblically literate or the biblically ignorant, communicated new information and invited the hearers to believe and change direction—in other words, to repent. Those who believed became learners. That is what disciples are. They started a process of reordering their lives and their beliefs based on the conviction that Jesus was the Christ, the saviour sent by God.

What new information does an African Muslim need to hear and believe in order to *start* being a disciple? The gospel is the good news of what God has done in Christ. What makes it *good* news to the hearer? When I ask workers what new information Muslims need to hear in order to make a decision to start following Jesus, they generally list doctrinal matters over which the gospel and Islam conflict. To be sure, all those matters need to be addressed at some point, but there is a world of difference between tackling them with someone who wants to follow and tackling them with someone who does not.

Some might say that faithfulness to the gospel requires us to address these areas of conflict first. However, in Acts, none of the messages started by correcting false belief; rather, they proclaimed news which made previous beliefs redundant. Acts is the only book in the New Testament in which we find examples of the Christian message being explicitly addressed to non-Christians. The Epistles were written to believers. Nowhere in Acts is the *necessity* of the cross expounded. Nowhere in Acts is the relationship between sacrifice and forgiveness explained. Nowhere in Acts is the nature of Christ discussed. Yet many believed and responded by changing their minds and starting to learn what it means to follow Christ. Often we have been conditioned to fill our messages to the unsaved with content drawn from the Epistles.

This observation does not mean that these subjects are not important, but it does demonstrate that they are not always obligatory for the initial presentation of the good news. In some contexts it may be good and right that these kinds of issues need to be addressed first, but that still means that it is the context that decides where our message has to start. To put it another way, the contents of our initial message about Christ should be tailored to the people who are being addressed.

We should expect that all messages that were developed in a significantly different context (such as our home country) will fail at some point when imported into a radically different context. This is true even of biblical passages; the model which we find demonstrated in Scripture is that speakers select their content according to the circumstances of the listener. We should not assume that Scripture will communicate simply because it is Scripture. To use a facile example, "You must be born again" will be heard to support reincarnation in the ears of someone who already holds that view.

During my time in Africa, I was continually seeking ways of communicating the good news about Christ that made sense to the listener and was sufficient to invite a response. I was looking for something that could be stated in two to three minutes when required, but could also be expanded to frame a whole dialogue.

I would like to share two messages here, not because they will be right for every context but rather to encourage others to attempt to develop their own. Both messages come under the Christus Victor approach to atonement and intentionally bypass contentious doctrinal issues.

The First Adam and the Second

We all know the first Adam. Do you know about the second? God created our father Adam and made him a perfect man. God put him in an ideal place. Adam heard the words of God with his own ears, glory to God. But Satan was stronger than our father Adam, and Satan deceived him and Adam went wrong. Because of that he fell, and in the end he died.

And the descendants of Adam became like him. They also did wrong, and it was easy for Satan to deceive them and ruin them. And they die. God sent them prophets to give them words of truth. But the children of Adam, like Adam, were not strong, and they could not follow the truth as they should; and it was easy for Satan to deceive them and ruin them. God gave rules, laws, and commandments. But the children of Adam are no stronger than their ancestor, and Satan easily leads them astray.

And so God sent the second Adam. His birth was different from that of the children of Adam. He had no human father. And he was strong and did no wrong. Satan was not able to deceive him. The second Adam defeated the devil and drove demons from people. He healed the sick and encouraged the poor. And his name is Isa al-Masih, glory to God.

> We are all children of Adam by our birth, and so we inherit his weakness. We can become brothers of the second Adam by faith, and he shares his strength with us. He offers us new life. God sent Jesus Christ to save us from Satan's power. The second Adam is alive. Believe in him and follow his way.

This approach echoes Paul's teaching about Christ and Adam in Romans 5:12–17 and 1 Corinthians 15:21–22 and 45–49. It describes the Fall in terms that Muslims recognise. Rather than correcting what is lacking in the Islamic account of the Fall, it draws out its implications. Indirectly, it challenges the standard Islamic message of salvation through obedience to laws by pointing to human experience.

It presents Christ as being in a way "like Adam" (an expression used in Islam, but with different connotations). It portrays Christ as being powerful and alive. It draws on the familiar to put together a new, unfamiliar message ("news") with immediate relevance. The terminology is so familiar that Muslims have been known to figure out that we are talking about Jesus before his name is used.

Although sin is mentioned, the approach does not talk about guilt so much as powerlessness. It resonates with those living with a power-fear paradigm.

Colleagues who work in Turkey tell me that the popular wisdom there is that people can always resist the evil if they really want to. In Africa, people are less optimistic and the presence, power, and threat of evil is ever present. This is a message that announces welcome news—that God has met a need they are deeply aware of. It provides a reason to start learning the truth about Christ. It can be expressed in two minutes or can be used as a mental road map for leading a group through a two-hour discussion.

There is nothing inherently individualistic in this message. It addresses a universal need with a God-given, universally available solution. It communicates a truth of value to all, but which can be appropriated by an individual.

Across Africa, Adam is one of the most popular names for boys. This is not true of the Middle East, the Turkish world, or further east. We might speculate as to why that would be, but the fact remains that it is a common name, and that fact alone creates opportunities to use this approach in everyday conversation.

The second message concerns *tahaara* ritual cleanliness or purity, something we find hard even to express in English because it has no place in Western culture. In many African and Muslim cultures, people are constantly aware of their level of ritual purity, a perception encouraged by Islamic practices.

Being Clean before God

How can God accept someone who is not clean? Being clean before God is vital.

A man with leprosy came to the Lord Jesus. At that time, a person with leprosy was considered unclean. He could never enter the place of prayer. He knelt before Jesus and said, "Heal me so that I will be clean."

And Jesus touched him and immediately the man became clean. Glory to God.

There was a woman who had been subject to bleeding for twelve years. She said to herself, "If I touch the clothes of Jesus, I will be well and become clean." She approached him and touched the hem of his garment.

Jesus turned and saw her. He said, "My daughter, take heart. Your faith in me has saved you." Right then she was completely healed and became clean. Glory to God.

Even if a person's body is healthy, he is not pure if his heart is unclean. Christ said, "What comes from inside a man, from his heart, that is what makes him unclean. For from inside a person—from his heart—come bad thoughts, wicked desires, theft, murder, adultery, greed, wickedness, deception, corruption, evil eye, slander, pride, and folly."

Can a man wash his own heart clean? No, he can't. But Christ is able to purify the heart of the person who believes in him. Glory to God.

Jesus Christ is alive and active. He does what no other can. Glory to God.

Is your heart clean? If not, how will you clean it?

97

While most Muslims do not wrestle with sinfulness, uncleanness is a constant preoccupation. This approach takes seriously the felt need of being clean. It identifies two examples of physical impurity which generally resonate, leprosy and blood, and draws on something that Muslims know—namely, that Jesus healed. It also draws on what they have not thought about— namely, that Jesus not only healed but also made clean with his touch.

This approach also adds the teaching of Jesus concerning the true nature of uncleanness—namely, sin proceeding from the heart. However, rather than unpacking atonement theology, it simply affirms that faith in Christ brings inner cleanness. There is enough here to encourage serious enquiry and a desire to learn.

The message can be delivered in two minutes, but the stories can of course be told at greater length with appropriate dramatisation. People remember and repeat stories that appeal to them.

Concern over how to be truly clean, the need of the heart, and the idea that a godly Sufi master may attain levels higher than the ordinary believer could ever achieve are all familiar in different expressions of Sufism found in Africa.

The nature of sin is addressed in terms of the true causes of uncleanness, not in terms of guilt, and this is done by quoting an impeccable source—Jesus himself—rather than a document. This resonates with many forms of the honour-shame paradigm and to some extent with the power-fear paradigm.

In addition, this presentation intentionally uses both male and female examples. In so doing it follows the example of Jesus in Matthew 13:31–33 and Luke 15:1–10. Ritual uncleanness is a big issue in the life of Muslim women. The direction the story takes may well surprise many Muslim women. They may expect Jesus to rebuke the woman! The story imparts hope. And that hope points them to Christ, the living saviour. It affirms that Christ is potentially able to save all who are aware of their need.

It is imperative that we develop gospel presentations that have a narrative that resonates with the culture and the sense of need that people have. While odd individuals may, for whatever reason, buy into a presentation that depends on alien thinking, they will not be able to pass it on to others, because their acceptance of the message is due to their own eccentricity, not to the universality of the message.

TASKS, REFLECTIONS, AND MATTERS TO DISCUSS

Explore how people express their separation from God. It might not be in absolute terms, but one powerful driver of religious practice is a sense of need.

Among themselves, do people see any deficiencies in their local religious system? What new ideas or teachers are being talked about within local Islam?

Make a list (and keep updating it) of what people already know that is helpful to us in announcing the good news. What do they know about God, about humanity, about religion, about commandments, about judgement, and about Jesus?

Find out if their culture celebrates any form of salvation or redemption in its stories.

Additional Resources

Bell, Steve. *Gospel for Muslims.* Milton Keynes, UK: Authentic, 2012.

https://sahelchurchplanter.wordpress.com/2018/06/26/good-news/.

"DOING CHURCH" IN MUSLIM AFRICA & PROXIMATE PEOPLES

In chapter 2, we met Pastor MC. He came to Christ in prison and began his discipleship in that relatively protected environment. On his release, he threw himself into the life of the church. Gambia is 90 percent Muslim. The church was made up of people of animist background who originated in neighbouring countries. MC was trained locally to be a pastor in the evangelical church, but he had no academic theological training.

MC found himself leading a typical African church in a solidly Muslim neighbourhood. He was disturbed to observe that the church had no impact on its neighbours. As time passed, he became increasingly discouraged. The style of worship grated on him. His church's lack of credibility with the Muslim majority troubled him. Confident that God was with him and that the Bible was true, he reasoned that there must be something wrong with the church.

He approached the denominational leadership and asked to be released from his duties to develop a new ministry. They refused. He accepted their refusal, but renewed his request regularly. Eventually they told him that if he really wanted to move away from the traditional role of pastor, he would have to forfeit his salary and his home. This he gladly accepted.

MC supported himself by working as a tailor living in the Fula quarter. Members of his extended family moved in with him, and he supported them. He did not preach at them, but developed patterns of regular prayer and worship in the Fula language. Some young men asked him to teach them. When the president of the church visited the house, he was so impressed that he became a supporter. MC went on to found a new style of church, along with a skills centre for dispossessed converts and a reconciliation ministry helping families to accept converts. He now heads a network that extends into several neighbouring countries. He has ploughed a new furrow.

I had the privilege of translating for Pastor MC in far-off Chad as he addressed a group of pastors and elders in the north of the country who found themselves serving a tiny minority of Christians drawn from traditionally animist peoples located in a Muslim-majority area. I found his story perversely encouraging, because it demonstrated that what was happening in Chad was not some local aberration. Right across the continent, we were wrestling with the same issues. Although major cultural commonalities are to be found across the Muslim and Christian populations, each religion develops them in different ways. The cultural barriers between typical Christian communities and typical Muslim populations are real and are usually reinforced by ethnicity and language differences. The close bond between ethnicity and religious identity guarantees it.

African Traditional Religions major on practices. There are beliefs behind the practices, but they are embedded in the subconscious worldview. Islam in Africa also majors on practices. You can be a very respectable Muslim with minimal understanding of the doctrines. Faith is something primarily expressed in terms of what you do.

The same pattern can be detected in many African churches. "We are the Christians, this is what we do, this is what Christians are." Being physically in the church meeting place and participating in church services is often central to the understanding of what it means to be a Christian. That does not necessarily mean that people do not hold firmly to Christian teaching, but it does mean that they do so because of who they belong to. It also means that the idea of changing their practices in order to take the message cross-culturally is an unfamiliar and unsettling idea. The notion that someone might belong to Christ but not be embedded in the visible Christian community is deeply counter-intuitive for African Christians. In many cases, their own history is one in which a whole people turned from the old rituals, the ancestors, and initiation to the new ways of church, Bible, and song book—along with the clinic and the school, of course.

There are reckoned to be over five hundred million people in Africa who describe themselves as Christians. The generalisations here are intentionally simplistic, but they are intended to alert workers to issues they might meet and to give an idea about how to start to interpret them.

Proximate Peoples

In many places, the churches see their mission as being to call people away from alcohol, immorality, and the occult and then keeping them safe from these evils. These are often very live issues within families and tribes. The Muslim communities also promote clean living. Many Christians will therefore feel it is not their business to be interfering with Muslims. After all, Christ came to call sinners to repentance.

Where Christians are in the majority, Muslims are usually not even on the radar. When individuals from such communities find themselves in Muslim-majority territory, their default option is to keep their heads down and to try not to draw attention to themselves.

Where Christians and Muslims live peacefully side by side, there is usually mutual respect, and harmony is defended. The status quo is maintained by willingly observing unspoken boundaries. Cross-boundary friendships may or may not occur, but conversions are rare.

Where Christians and Muslims live side by side with tension and mistrust, all interaction is affected. Churches often adopt a defensive posture, and seekers are regarded with deep suspicion. The Muslim authorities warn their followers to avoid being contaminated by the non-Muslims in their midst.

Where Christians are in a confident majority, it is not uncommon for foreign sectarian influences to find opportunity to form aggressive Christian subgroups. Here I am not primarily referring to heretical sects, but rather to some evangelical and Pentecostal groups. Such groups align themselves against the local orthodoxy and evangelise with energy. They may have right on their side, as regards the doctrinal issues, but they are often flawed in their spirituality. Such groups will be strident with regard to Muslims, especially within areas where Christians are strong. However, the energy of their members and their missionaries tends to die when they move into the Muslim heartlands. Part of their stridency involves stirring up fear, and fear is no basis for serious mission.

What then of the strategy of mobilising "proximate peoples" for the harvest? Obviously it is a sensible and practical way to go. However, outsiders often come along with a clear plan on paper that does not match the realities on the ground. They underestimate what kind of mental and emotional journey proximate peoples may have to make and overestimate the power of outsiders to bring it about. Outsiders arrive with an agenda that they see as rooted in Scripture and backed with divine authority. They assume that genuinely spiritual people will recognise it.

African leaders live in a more complex world, and they have their own more complex, relational agendas. They have their own approach to time and task. They lead whole communitarian churches, not narrow mission splinter groups. And it is not their custom to lay out in explicit detail what they are thinking. These circumstances provide the conditions within which misunderstandings multiply. Where partnerships are formed between church leaders and foreign missions, it is common for each party to actually be pursuing a quite different agenda.

The power balance is complex too. The outsiders are people of resources, technology, wealth, and impressive access to knowledge. The church leaders have the power to grant access and support visa applications. They also have extensive local knowledge. Who is the patron and who is the client? If both are both, then who makes the decisions? And how are decisions made?

Alternatively, missions coming in from outside can extract workers from the church. They are unlikely to think of what they are doing in those terms, but that is what they do. Paid African workers can be trained in the wisdom of the West (or increasingly the East) and can learn to function in the foreign agency. Unless they are exceptional individuals, the general public they are deployed to reach will correctly identify them as hired men (see John 10:12–13). As they blend into the new organisation, they are likely to lose their distinctiveness. Where their voice does not resonate with the view of the agency as a whole, they are ignored. And as dependents, they either accept that and change or they resent it and become disillusioned.

I once met a group of American mission leaders on a survey trip looking at the potential for ministry to Arabic speakers in Africa. They brought with them a Syrian Christian who was about fifty years old. The Americans were confident and vocal; the Syrian spoke when he was spoken to. His body language indicated to anyone who cared to look that he was not at all happy with much of what he heard. But he was circumspect. He was a dependent. When I spoke to him alone, he was always respectful, but he showed his misgivings about the whole project with dark hints. The other members of the party did not seem to notice. This pattern is repeated many times over when foreign missions hire non-Western expertise and all the power stays with the Westerners.

Is all this needlessly pessimistic? Perhaps. To put it another way, for the recruitment of local workers by zealous agencies, the agencies have to choose well, then a disciplined effort must be made to give the local workers space to speak and be heard. Decision makers have to form deep and trusting relationships with their dependent workers for the potential benefit to be attained.

Foreign Preoccupations and African Realities

Schooled in current thinking on church planting, many workers today dream of planting a genuine house-church movement. After all, the early church did not have buildings. Institutional development is a well-documented hindrance to multiplication. Where the gospel really takes off, house-church movements are often the result. Surely, it is said, a movement operating at the level of the home will be more truly at home in the culture than one revolving around the introduction of church buildings. All these arguments are basically true and valid, but the host culture is not a blank sheet waiting to be written on.

In my experience, Muslims in Africa, thinking and feeling within their culture, are strongly drawn to the idea of having a church building. They have a sensitivity to place and the use of space that outsiders do not have. Their homes have lines of demarcation in them that the non-African does not usually notice. Muslims may pray in their homes, but in certain places and under certain conditions. Prayer in a mosque is to be preferred; and setting up a special space, often just outside the home, is often what they do. Whatever the official legal status of a home, it is not private property in the way a Western home is. For a home to become the meeting place of people who are not kin involves adjustments to the arrangement of public and private space—not that there are only these two categories.

In my admittedly limited experience, I have noticed profound differences between the living arrangements of Christians of recent animist background as opposed to Muslims with centuries of Islam. Neither group is inclined to turn their homes into a public meeting place. Sufi sheikhs may be an important and, for our discussion, significant exception, for they build their home life around their ministry. But even they do not run an open home, as such. The organisation of space is important to them. A successful sheikh will have a space set aside for worship and teaching outside his private quarters and will use both in different ways. To be sure, the home must be a place where the gospel is expressed and lived, but that does not mean it will be the natural place for believers to congregate.

Whatever the underlying reasons, Africans like to have dedicated space for spiritual purposes. One might respond that this is because they need teaching, that they are thinking according to the flesh and that once enlightened they will see things differently. This sets up a powerful contradiction. If the aim is to plant a movement within the culture, how can one so casually reject selected subconscious features of it? If meeting in homes is made a primary commandment on a level with the Muslim obligatory washing before prayer, the cultural preference might be overcome. Whether it can be sustained is another matter. Muslims no longer live in communities isolated from the world. They know Muslims have mosques and Christian have church buildings. It is a bold ambition to attempt to expunge general knowledge.

While the biblical examples are home-related, there is no insistence that the home is uniquely appropriate as a meeting place for followers of Christ. What about the recorded observations of multiplication movements?

I think it is true to say that when there are rapidly growing, highly energised movements, especially in a contested environment, house-based activities are the norm. However, that is an observation of what occurs, not of the causes. It is still less a measure of people's aspirations. Generally, when such movements become established they start setting apart buildings. The home-level activity is a response to pressured circumstances, not a key to growth.

It has become an article of church-planting orthodoxy that church-planting workers should set aside all notions of what church should look like, which are derived from their home experience, and instead go back to the essentials of Scripture. Existing structures and organisations in any particular country are assumed to be part of the problem rather than part of the solution.

There is much wisdom in this approach. However, it is a fantasy to imagine that workers from outside will be the sole source of information about what following Christ means and what church is. Some workers, pursuing the goal of planting a movement in a particular group, act as if no other Christians exist. The implicit denial of what local people know to be true sets up a question that the strategy does not believe in answering. This nonverbal model speaks a confusing message and diminishes the gospel, which not only speaks of individual salvation but also of Christ calling together a people from every tribe and tongue. Authentic teaching of the gospel must always include an account of our connectedness to the global body of Christ. Although this is complicated and messy, it enhances the message, because a global message is taken, by definition, as more authoritative than a purely local or individual one.

Another approach that has become popular of late is to see church planters as people who simply give exposure to the good news and access to the Scriptures. They then allow the group of new believers to make all the culturally sensitive decisions. The forms of worship, the patterns of prayer, family life, and so on will be worked out by the believers guided by the Spirit.

In principle, this is sound enough as far as it goes. I suspect, however, that it is accompanied by a desire to avoid getting too entangled with people. It is true that the Apostle Paul kept moving and did not dig in for a long stay. It is also true that he was operating within his own culture, found converts who already had significant scriptural knowledge, often left juniors to supervise at least for a time, and returned to deal with deviations from the pattern he had established. Again and again he referred to himself and his team as models to be emulated, not merely as those who imparted some principles to be applied. They established patterns of worship and prayer. The testimony of Scripture is that the church planter is a model as well as a communicator. See, for example, Acts 20:18–35; 1 Corinthians 11:1, 16; Philippians 3:17; 1 Thessalonians 2:9–14.

Islam has taken root in Africa and is extending itself primarily through activists and followers presenting themselves as a model to follow. They never attempt to teach a set of principles for new Muslims to apply nor teach them an approach to interpreting the Qur'an in order to resolve issues that may come up. Granted, the spiritual dynamic in Islam is not Christian and the Bible is not the Qur'an. Muslims have no Holy Spirit to depend on.

That said, part of the success of Islam in Africa comes from working with the culture. Beliefs are taught through patterns of behaviour. Teachers are assumed to be examples in every part of life. Seekers and believers relate to people, not principles. Authority is accessible in embodied living people seen to be connected to other people. That is not significantly different from the practice of the early church.

The Apostle Paul once posed the question, "Who is equal to such a task?" (2 Cor 2:16). His answer comes a few verses later. "Not that we are competent in ourselves to claim anything for ourselves, but our competence comes from God. He has made us competent as ministers of a new covenant—not of the letter but of the Spirit; for the letter kills, but the Spirit gives life" (2 Cor 3:5–6).

TASKS, REFLECTIONS, AND MATTERS TO DISCUSS

If there are African Christians in your area, find out what attitude they show towards Muslims.

If your organisation has African co-workers, what can you learn from them?

Do you have a partnership with an African church? If so, try to assess whether its leaders really understand your agenda. Do you understand and sympathise with theirs?

Does your team have a clear idea of what Muslim-convert churches should look like? If not, why not? If yes, where does that idea come from?

To what extent are you and your team a suitable model for future new believers?

CPSIA information can be obtained
at www.ICGtesting.com
Printed in the USA
BVHW042319151219
566784BV00005B/13/P

3 4711 00233 9861

9 781645 082521